*When Adam Clarke Preached,*
*People Listened*

# WHEN ADAM CLARKE

## PREACHED

## *PEOPLE LISTENED*

Studies in the Message and Method of
Adam Clarke's Preaching

by
Wesley Tracy

Beacon Hill Press of Kansas City
Kansas City, Missouri

I am my dr Mr E

yours affy

A Clarke

Copyright 1981
Beacon Hill Press of Kansas City

ISBN: 0-8341-0714-7

Printed in the United States of America

Dedicated to the memory of
my father,
REV. D. H. TRACY,
who taught me to appreciate Christian
preaching and introduced me to
the writings of Adam Clarke

# Contents

## Introduction

# Welcome Back, Adam

"My heart is with you," declared the 72-year-old Adam Clarke to his friends gathered around a London fireside in 1832, "and when my spirit has passed away—if God permits—it shall return, and be a stirring spirit among you again."[1]

A few months later, Adam Clarke, the man who taught the Methodists how to study the Bible, preached full salvation to them for 52 years, and all the while demonstrated how personal religion and social concern go together, died a victim of the 1832 cholera epidemic. He was buried next to John Wesley at City Road Chapel by mourning Methodists.

It is my prayerful hope that this book can help make Clarke's prediction a fulfilled prophecy. I hope this volume can release the spirit and vitality of Adam Clarke to be a "stirring spirit" among us again. May we find the fervent spirit of Adam Clarke walking the corridors of our collective heart, awakening us to the vitality of our Wesleyan heritage of scriptural holiness. Then we shall all gladly say, "Welcome back, Adam Clarke."

Through these pages it is hoped that Adam Clarke will coach the reader to better understand, own, and celebrate his or her Wesleyan heritage, and grasp anew what it means to be a Wesleyan today.

This book is also about preaching. Clarke was a great preacher; in an era of pulpit giants he "out-congregationed" them all. We know about his commentary. When I started preaching 25 years ago, you had to have a set of "Clarke"—even if you couldn't afford a Bible. Some people know of his *Christian Theology*. But far fewer have even heard of his preaching. He preached some 15,000 sermons. But he preached them all without manuscript or notes. Most of them have been proclaimed, done their work upon the hearts of those who were privileged to hear him, and are gone forever. However, 19 of his sermons were taken down in shorthand as he preached them. And another 41 sermons are ours because, in response to popular demand, Clarke went back to the study after he had preached them, and wrote out these sermons for publication.

Upon discovering these sermons, I enthusiastically embraced this nearly lost piece of our heritage. In these 60 sermons Clarke has been teaching me about what it means to be a Wesleyan. Further, by his example, he is teaching me how to preach better. If you want to enroll in the same class, please turn the page. I hope you will find that Adam Clarke's "stirring spirit" is there.

# 1

# Adam Who?

The meeting house at St. Austell was already jammed with eager hearers. Although the young Methodist preacher, Adam Clarke, arrived more than half an hour early, he couldn't get in—and he was to be the speaker. The house was filled, even the balcony was bulging, and the crowd so filled the front yard that there was no hope of getting to the door. Adam made his way to the side of the building and worked his way through the crowd at the window nearest the pulpit. Tucking his Bible into his coat, he climbed in the window and, literally crawling over the heads and shoulders of the jam-packed crowd, made his way to the pulpit.

This was an exercise the young preacher was to get used to. Again and again he had to use some such ingenious method to get to the pulpit as for 52 years the people of England and Ireland flocked to hear him preach. They did not come out to hear a flamboyant spellbinder, a flaming evangelist, or a silver-tongued orator. No, Adam Clarke was an expositor of the Word; he was the Bible teacher of adolescent Methodism.

"If God has given me one gift," he said, "it is the gift of explaining the scriptures."[1] He was a man of one message—a message he found throughout the Bible.

Many today know Clarke through his commentary or his *Christian Theology,* but few are aware that he was a preacher larger than life in an era of giants. Samuel Drew, a younger contemporary of Clarke, said that Clarke drew larger audiences for a longer period of time than any man in the history of Christianity.[2]

But what of the sermons that moved Britain to the foot of the Cross for half a century? As already noted, Clarke preached some 15,000 times, but he never took a manuscript or even an outline to the pulpit with him. Thus these thousands of sermons are lost forever—almost. Forty-one of his sermons were published after the fact. That is, by popular demand Clarke went to his study and wrote out these sermons for publication after he had preached them. These, along with the 19 which were taken down in shorthand as he preached are all that we have—60 out of 15,000 sermons. But those 60 sermons constitute a vital part of our heritage which can be reborn in us with great profit. And that's what this book is about—the powerful preaching of Adam Clarke.

But before we can properly understand what a man says, and how he says it, we must know who he is. What of this towering personality of early Methodism?

## THE CHILDHOOD OF ADAM CLARKE

As a small boy in school in Northern Ireland, Adam Clarke was a dismal student. The class was working through *Lily's Latin Grammar.* Young Adam worked for two and a half days; but when called upon to recite the first lesson in class, he could not remember two lines. The schoolmaster dealt with this learning difficulty by declaring for everyone to hear, "If you do not speedily get that lesson, I shall pull your ears as long as Jowler's" (a big hound which stayed around the school), "and you shall be a beggar till the day of your death." Adam's classmates greeted him with the chorus of "What a stupid ass."[3]

"Shall I ever be a dunce, and the butt of these fellows' insults?" the mortified boy said to himself.[4] He grabbed his book and learned the lesson forthwith.

That was only a small breakthrough in the matter of learning. Adam repeatedly failed in his father's own school which he and his older brother Tracy took turns attending. While one lad was in their father's classroom, the other was at home working on the farm the family rented. Adam proved insufferably dull—it looked like ploughing and peat cutting would be his career. Adam's father, a strict disciplinarian, could not teach him. "His voice was a terror to me," Adam recalled. "It nearly broke my heart to perceive that my efforts to learn were fruitless. I wandered in the fields and sighed and wept and still kept dogging at it, but could not get on."[5]

Then one day a visiting teacher came to class with Adam's father. He examined some of the students with rather good results. Mr. John Clarke, the resident teacher, beamed with pride. Then it was Adam's turn. John Clarke explained apologetically, "That boy is slow at learning. I fear you will not be able to do much with him." Adam, recalling the incident, wrote, "My heart sank. I would have given the world to have been as some of the boys around me."[6]

The now unknown visiting teacher, however, took some time with young Adam, spoke kindly to him, gave him some directions, and, laying his hand on his head, observed, "This lad will make a good scholar yet."[7]

Adam Clarke said, "I felt this kindness. It raised my spirit. . . . a ray of hope sprang up within me. . . . It seemed to create power. My lessons were all committed to memory with ease."[8]

Clarke later wrote that "encouragement and kind words from the teacher are indispensably necessary [to learning]. . . . The mildest methods are the most likely to be efficient. The smallest progress should be . . . commended that it may excite to farther . . . diligence."[9]

A third liberation of Clarke's mental powers came at his conversion, of which change Samuel Dunn said, "He now learned more in one day than formerly he was able to do in one month."[10] Through these steps the scholarly gifts of Clarke, which illuminate the Christian paths of many yet today, were revealed and enhanced.

When Adam Clarke was born, the family lived in the hamlet of Maybeg in Londonderry County, Ireland. His ancestors were English and Scottish but had lived in Ireland for several generations. The family at one time had rather large landholdings near Larne and Glenarme in Ireland, but by Adam's time they had been stripped of every acre. Adam was born in 1760 or 1762. His parents could never agree on the exact year. Adam himself said it was 1760.

John Clarke, Adam's father, was a highly educated man, being trained for the ministry at Edinburgh, Glasgow, and Trinity College, Dublin. But church appointments never came. He became a teacher and was never financially successful.

Adam's mother, whose maiden name was Boyd, was Scottish. She was a Presbyterian and was concerned for the religious training of her children. Adam said, "For my mother's religious teachings I shall have endless reason to bless my Maker."[11] She taught her children the catechism by memory. She studied the Bible and taught it to the children. She also taught her children to pray. They knelt one at a time by her knee every night and repeated the Lord's Prayer, then (those above six) repeated the Apostles' Creed before imploring blessings on all the family members and close friends. The ceremony ended with the evening prayer, followed by a short doxology. The children then greeted the daybreak with the morning prayer.

The morning prayer was:

> *Preserve me, Lord, amidst the crowd,*
> *From every thought that's vain and proud;*
> *And raise my wandering mind to see*
> *How good it is to trust in Thee.*
> *From all the enemies of Thy truth,*
> *Do Thou, O Lord, preserve my youth;*
> *And raise my mind from worldly cares,*
> *From youthful sins and youthful snares.*
> *Lord, though my heart's as hard as stone,*
> *Let seeds of early grace be sown,*
> *Still watered by Thy heavenly love,*
> *Till they spring up in joys above.*

The evening prayer was:

> *I go to my bed as to my grave,*
> *And pray to God my life to save;*
> *But if I die before I wake,*
> *I pray the Lord my soul to take.*
> *Sweet Jesus, now to Thee I cry,*
> *To grant me mercy ere I die;*
> *To grant me mercy, and send me peace,*
> *That heaven may be my dwelling-place.*[12]

Adam's mother's teachings stressed the justice of God to the near exclusion of His mercy. The children (there were seven) dreaded God. When the children misbehaved, she whipped out the Bible and read a condemning text in accusative tones which terrified the children. One day Adam disobeyed his mother and gave her a hateful look and gesture at the same time. She flew to the Bible and read Prov. 30:17, "The eye that mocketh at his father, and despiseth to obey his mother, the ravens of the valley shall pick it out." The young culprit was cut to the heart, believing the words were sent straight from heaven to him. Under this cloud he went out into the field to ponder his denounced waywardness. A "hoarse croak of a raven sounded to his conscience an alarm more terrible than the cry of fire at midnight!"[13] Spying the bird, he knew its mission of divine vengeance was to pick out his two eyes. Shrieking in repentance and terror, he clapped both hands over his eyes and ran for the house. "My mother's reproofs and terrors never left me," Adam confessed, "till I sought and found the salvation of God."[14]

Besides the formal education in school and the religious education at home, young Adam received an informal education in life. He was a hardworking farmhand from the age of six. He enjoyed the outdoor sports of the Irish countryside. Horsemanship, swimming, and fishing were among his favorite activities. He also enjoyed the sports of the local gatherings such as "putting the stone, weightlifting, and balancing."[15] The youthful Adam was skilled in the latter. In this game anything was balanced in the hand: crowbars, sledgehammers, even ladders.

Young Adam enjoyed the company of several playmates. Their names seem to conjure up an interesting and normal boyhood. His chums included lads called: Goat, Turkey, Pigmy Will, and Tithe. The latter's real name was James Brooks, but he carried the nickname Tithe because he was the 10th child in the family. When he was old enough to walk, his mother took him to church and gave him to the minister as a tithe of her children. The good parson kept the child and raised him. Seeking help in rearing large families was not uncommon in those days. Adam himself was once sent to his grandparents to live, but he played so recklessly that he twice nearly drowned in the well, so his grandparents sent him back.

Adam developed an intense interest in reading. Among his childhood favorites were *Robin Hood, The Battle of the Boyne, Robinson Crusoe, Pilgrim's Progress, Aesop's Fables, Nine Worthies of the World, Don Quixote, Seven Champions of Christendom, Babes in the Woods, Rochester's Poems,* and *The Arabian Nights.* The latter marked the beginning of an interest in Asian and Middle Eastern lore which ended with his mastering several ancient languages.

Adam's informal excursions into various fields of knowledge sometimes proved to be about as profitable as planting dandelions. He developed an interest and read widely in astrology, alchemy, witchcraft, magic, and spiritualism. He even had his young friends believing he could cast spells. During the period when he was reading works in this area, a fortune-teller was a guest in the Clarke home. He was asked to tell the future of the young Adam. He told Adam and the rest of the family that the child would grow up and become a fat drunkard, with an enormous belly. Adam fled the scene and hid in the furze bushes and prayed that such a plight would never befall him—it didn't. Adam soon gave up his inquiries into magic and its related evils.

As a young teen Adam enrolled in a music class. He tolerated the theoretical instruction in order to enjoy the dancing which always followed the lesson. Adam soon came to love dancing like a begonia loves sunshine. He later wrote of this experience, concluding that dancing was "a perverting influence and an unmixed moral evil."[16]

## ADAM CLARKE, MEET THE MASTER

In 1777, when the U.S.A. was a year-old nation, the Methodists began to preach in the Irish parish of Agherton where the Clarkes lived. The first Methodist preacher Adam ever heard was one John Bretell, who was preaching in a barn. Clarke did not remember the text nor much of the sermon. But he did remember that Bretell had declared that no matter what the Westminster Confession says, the Bible teaches present salvation from all sin.[17]

A Methodist preacher named Thomas Barber soon began to evangelize throughout the whole region, preaching in houses, barns, schools, and in the open air. The whole Clarke family heard him, took him into their home at times, and approved of his doctrine. Young Adam went to every service within walking distance in which Barber preached. He averaged hearing Thomas Barber four times a week. This, in addition to some personal counsel from Barber, soon awoke in Adam a seeking spirit. He yearned to have the assurance of present salvation.

Adam began to attend the Methodist society meetings in Mullihicall. One day the leader of the society, Andrew Hunter of Coleraine, spoke to Adam in a most affectionate way about giving his whole heart to God, for "you may be a burning and shining light in a benighted land."[18] These words pierced Clarke to the heart, and conviction increased and persisted day and night. One morning in 1778 he went to work in the field which his father rented between Port Stuart and Coleraine. Typifying the reticence of those days to give personal illustrations directly, Adam Clarke tells his own story of that day in the third person:

> One morning, in great distress of soul, he went out to his work in the field. He began, but could not proceed, so great was his mental anguish. He fell down on his knees on the earth, and prayed; but seemed to be without power or faith. He arose and endeavored

18

to work, but could not; even his physical strength seemed to have departed from him. He again endeavored to pray; but the gates of heaven appeared as if barred against him. His faith in the atonement, so far as it concerned himself, was almost entirely gone; he could not believe that Jesus had died *for him;* the thickest darkness seemed to gather round and settle on his soul. He fell flat on his face on the earth, and endeavored to pray, but still there was no answer: he arose, but he was so weak that he could scarcely stand.

His agonies were indescribable: he seemed to be for ever separated from God and the glory of his power. Death, in any form, he could have preferred to his present feelings, if that death could put an end to them. No fear of hell produced those terrible conflicts. He had not God's approbation; he had not God's image. He felt that without a sense of his favor he could not live. Where to go, what to say, and what to do, he found not: even the words of prayer at last failed; he could neither plead nor wrestle with God. . . .

It is said, the time of man's extremity is the time of God's opportunity. He now felt "Come to the Holiest through the blood of Jesus." He looked up, confidently, to the Savior of sinners. His agony subsided, his soul became calm. A glow of happiness thrilled through his frame; all guilt and condemnation were gone. He examined his conscience, and found it no longer a register of sins against God. He looked to heaven, and all was sunshine; he searched for his distress, but could not find it. He felt indescribably happy, but could not tell the cause: a change had taken place within him of a nature wholly unknown before, and for which he had no name.

He sat down upon the ridge where he had been working, full of ineffable delight. He praised God. His physical strength returned, and he could bound like a roe. He had felt a sudden transition from darkness to light, from guilt and oppressive fear to confidence and peace. He could now draw nigh to God with more confidence than he could to his earthly father: he had freedom of access, and freedom of speech. He was like a person who had got into a new world, where, although

19

> every object was strange, yet each was pleasing; and now he could magnify God for his creation, a thing he never could do before. O, what a change was here![19]

The born-again Adam Clarke quickly became a "burning and shining light in a benighted land." He went from village to village, sharing his faith. His usual method was to call at a home and ask the family members if he could have prayer with them. The answer was always yes, according to Clarke. He then asked the husband or wife of the family to invite any neighbors they wished to join them. When all were assembled, Adam read from the Scriptures, led a hymn, testified about "experimental religion" and the awfulness of sin, and led the group in prayers. He then departed quickly en route to another such meeting. He visited as many as 10 villages in a day in this manner.

Adam's conversion also transformed the family life at the Clarke home. He soon became the leader of family devotions for the family of nine. Most of his relatives also felt his influence and became members of the Connexion.

But the practical concerns of life soon impinged upon these happy scenes. Adam was nearing the age of 20 with no career in sight. His parents first wanted him to become an Anglican priest, then a medical doctor like his older brother Tracy. But all the family funds had been drained sending Tracy to school. Adam said his parents always spoiled Tracy and that he never recovered from it. Perhaps he was right—after getting his medical degree, Tracy took a job as medical doctor on a slave ship. Finally it was decided Adam should go into business, and he was sent as an apprentice to Mr. Bennett of Coleraine and Dublin, a relative in the Irish linen business. He got along well in this business; but when Bennett insisted that he cut the linen several inches short of a yard and stretch it to 36 inches, Adam resigned.

About this time he became acquainted with Mr. Bredin, one of the Methodist preachers on the Londonderry circuit. Bredin made him an occasional helper on the circuit and urged him to preach. Although Adam had exhorted many times, he had never taken a text and preached. This was a sacred and fearful thing to him. Finally he yielded, and at the village of New Buildings on June 19, 1779, he preached his first sermon from the text "We know that we are of God, and the whole world lieth in wickedness" (1 John 5:19). During the next two weeks by popular demand he preached five more times, and a new vocation loomed before him. He now had a strong persuasion that he was called to preach. The call was confirmed when the verse was strongly impressed upon him which reads, "Ye have not chosen me, but I have chosen you, and ordained you, that ye should go and bring forth fruit" (John 15:16).

Through Mr. Bredin he soon received an invitation from John Wesley to come to England and attend Kingswood School to train for the ministry. Having prayerfully made up his mind that it was God's will, he set out for home to report the good news.

When he announced to his parents that he intended to become an itinerant Methodist preacher, they couldn't stand it. His father would neither speak to him nor remain in a room where Adam was. His mother threatened him with divine and parental curses. She declared:

> We have brought you up with much care and trouble; your brother is gone, your father cannot last always, you should stay with the family, and labour for the support of those who have so long supported you, and not go to be a fugitive and vagabond over the face of the earth. I believe you to be upright, I know you to be godly; but remember God has said, *Honour thy father and thy mother; that thy days may be long in the land which the Lord thy God giveth thee*. This is

21

the *first commandment with promise:* and remember what the apostle hath said, *Whosoever shall keep the whole law, and yet offend in one point, is guilty of all.* Now, I allow that you are unblamable in your life, but you are now going to break that solemn law, *Honour thy father and thy mother;* and if you do, what will avail all your other righteousness? . . . If you go, you shall have a parent's curse, and not her blessing.[20]

Adam was in a dilemma. He sought God faithfully. He left home for a few days on family business and upon his return found his parents in a better mood. His mother, while praying, had become convinced that she must give up her son. She, with some effort, convinced her husband of the same. They were not exactly happy with the prospect that the son who should care for them in their old age was going to be a poor Methodist preacher, but they had become reconciled to it.

## THE KINGSWOOD ORDEAL

From Ireland, Adam traveled to Bristol, England. He then walked the remaining four miles to Kingswood School. Full of high hopes of finding a "chimerical Utopia and garden of paradise"[21] where he could increase his learning and piety, Adam found the headmaster, Mr. Simpson, and presented the letter from John Wesley. It soon became evident that the Kingswood staff had never heard of freshman orientation or even public relations.

Simpson told him that he knew nothing of his coming, that there were no empty rooms, and that Mr. Wesley was away and would not be back for two weeks. "You must go back to Bristol and lodge there till he comes," he told him.

Poor Adam had spent all his money for passage and had only three half-pence to his name. Upon telling Simpson this, he was challenged with, "Why would *you* come to Kingswood? It is only for preachers' children, or for such preachers as cannot read their Bibles, . . . from this information . . . you read both Greek and Latin."[22]

Finally Simpson agreed that there was one spare room away from the house and the school, on the end of the chapel. The room had no heat, scarcely any bedding, and little furniture. Adam was told he was to stay in that room day and night. He was not to come to class, chapel, or meals. His food and water would be brought by a servant.

He finally discovered the reason for his isolation: He was Irish, and thus they supposed he would have the itch. Finding this out, he took off his shirt and showed the headmaster that he had no such disease. He was then informed that it might still be "cleaving" to him and that he would not be allowed out of his room until he had rubbed himself from head to toe with Jackson's Itch Ointment. Clarke wrote,

> . . . and with this infernal ungent I was obliged to anoint myself before a large fire, (the first and last I saw while I remained there,) which they had ordered to be lighted for the purpose. In this state, smelling worse than a polecat, I tumbled with a heavy heart and streaming eyes into my worthless bed. The next morning the sheets had taken from my body, as far as they came in contact with it, the unabsorbed parts of this tartereous compound: and the smell of them and myself was almost insupportable. The woman that brought my *bread and milk* for breakfast, for dinner, and for supper,—I begged to let me have a pair of clean sheets. It was in vain: no clean clothes of any kind were afforded me; . . . For more than three weeks no soul performed any kind act for me.[23]

Finally on September 6, 1782, after Adam had experienced many more indignities, especially at the hand of Mrs. Simpson, from whom he ran like a man pursued by a tiger, John Wesley returned to Bristol, and Adam was called to meet him in Wesley's study in Broodmead Chapel. John Wesley received him kindly and after a short,

23

informal discussion asked him, "Well, Brother Clarke, do you wish to devote yourself entirely to the work of God?" Adam answered, "Sir, I wish to *do* and *be* what God pleases."

Wesley replied, "We want a preacher for Bradford-Wilts, hold yourself in readiness to go . . . I . . . will let you know when you shall go." He then laid his hands upon Adam's head and prayed an ordination prayer in which he asked God to *bless, preserve,* and give him *success* in the work to which he was called.[24]

## ADAM CLARKE: A MODEL MINISTER

For the next 52 years Adam Clarke was a hardworking Methodist preacher. Most of those years he spent in circuit preaching. The latter years he spent primarily in writing, traveling in the superintendency, and serving as a leader in various conference-wide Methodist concerns.

Hard work was his trademark; he was determined not to join the "already ample company of the slothful servants and religious loungers in the Lord's inheritance."[25] The first circuit he served (Bradford-Wilts) had 32 chapels and preaching points. Four ministers and one horse served this circuit. In Adam's first year (really 10½ months) he preached 506 sermons. During his itinerancy he served 11 different circuits. During his first tour of duty in London he walked over 7,000 miles going to preaching appointments. Because he taught himself French in his "free" time, he was assigned to the Norman Isles for three years, where he had good success.

He was an overwhelmingly popular preacher. Frequently the meetinghouses were filled hours before the time of service. Young people were particularly attracted to him. On several occasions he would arrive at the church to find such a mass that he could hardly get into the building. More than once he had to enter a side window and literally crawl on hands and knees over the heads and shoulders of the people to reach the pulpit. On at least three occasions the churches in which he was preaching were so overcrowded that the balconies sagged and cracked and disaster threatened.

Adam was not content to be a pleaser of multitudes. He was a shepherd, a pastor at heart. One of his most distinguished services was his ministry to the sick and dying. His concern for the poor was constant, as we shall explore later. His pastoral calls were many, and he always shared whatever food his poor parishioners offered him. He preached at 5:00 in the morning summer and winter in order to reach persons on their way to work. Some of his parishioners complained that they couldn't get up in time to attend these street-side services, so Adam at 4 a.m. walked through the streets with a lantern, banging on doors and getting people out of bed in time for the service. He preached in the chapels and streets, called in the homes, cared for the poor, visited the sick, organized societies, attended the class meetings, and dealt skillfully with matters of practical administration.

Many incidents could be cited to show his pastoral skills, but let the case of Mr. Selbey of Manchester serve as a singular example. Selbey had been first a boxer, then a gambler, then a cockfighter, and all the while a drunkard. Then he was converted in a Methodist meeting, and God delivered him from that miserable life. He had much to praise God for and couldn't keep from it. His "hallelujahs" disturbed every service—even the society meetings and the love feasts. Finally the local congregation had had enough. They would lock him out. The next congregational meeting was a love feast. They wouldn't let him in. Selbey just knelt outside the door praying, listening at the keyhole for some word of blessing. When the service dismissed, some persons tried to console the shut-out Selbey, but no complaint came from him. As the quiet-treasuring members came out, Selbey was still rejoicing and greeted them all with praises to God, all in a simple, good spirit. "Glory be to God!" he exclaimed. "I could hear that the Lord was among you."

When Adam Clarke, a minister on the circuit, heard what had happened, he cancelled his plans for study and went out to the humble home of the joyful ex-drunkard and his wife and spent half a day visiting, talking about the Bible and spiritual things. Thereafter, he was a frequent visitor to the Selbey hut. One asked him later if he did not think that Selbey was deranged. "No more, Sir, than you are," Clarke replied; "he may be an annoyance to some preachers, but he helps me. I would not have been the person to have prevented that good man from enjoying the ordinances of God—no, not for the whole world."[26]

The duties of preaching and pastoring, however thoroughly done, did not keep Adam Clarke from intense study and scholarly achievement. He practiced what he preached concerning good use of time. He wrote to a preacher, "The grand secret is to save time; spend none needlessly; keep from all unnecessary company; . . . and have, as often as possible, a book in your hand. Do not lie long in bed, nor sit up late at night. . . . Study yourself *half* to death, and pray yourself *whole* to life."[27]

Clarke was a lifelong learner. He delved in many areas of study, including medicine, chemistry, and mineralogy. He learned some 20 languages, including Greek, Hebrew, Latin, Persian, and Aramaic. Biblical studies consumed more study time than anything else. He translated the entire Bible from the original tongues before starting his *Commentary.* He was probably the most able biblical scholar of his time in the English-speaking world.

He was a voluminous author with works too numerous

to list. Among his most distinguished ones were: *The Bibliographic Dictionary,* six volumes (an elaborate chronological annotated account of the most rare and important books from all departments of literature); *Succession of Sacred Literature . . . to the Year of Our Lord 1445;* his work for the Crown on Rhymers *Foedera;* and of course his six-volume *Commentary on the Holy Scriptures.*

His many honors included: two honorary degrees from the University of Aberdeen, membership in the Royal Asiatic Society, the Antiquarian Society, the London Geological Society, the Royal Irish Academy, the American Antiquarian Society, and the Eclectic Society. He was librarian for the Surrey Institute, subcommissioner of the Public Records for the King, and president of the Philological Societies of Liverpool and Manchester. Not the least of his honors was being elected three times as president of the Methodist Connexion. In those days it was unheard of for a lowly Methodist preacher to be so widely acclaimed.

Clarke was an innovative leader. Almost single-handedly he planted Methodism in the Shetland Islands. He established schools for the poor Irish children on his own. He led Methodist antislavery activities and probably raised more money for missions, the British and Foreign Bible Society, and the Sunday Schools than any three other men of his time.

## Husband and Father

Adam Clarke made the acquaintance of Mary Cooke, the daughter of a successful clothing merchant of Trowbridge. They corresponded for some time—mostly about theological concerns. Love finally blossomed and Adam and Mary planned to get married. Mary's parents had higher hopes for their daughter than a marriage to a Methodist preacher eking out a meager existence in the Norman Isles. So vigorous was their opposition that Mary's mother appealed to John Wesley. Wesley wrote to Adam and informed him that if he married Miss Cooke without her mother's permission, he would dismiss him from the Methodist Connexion. Permission was finally given, and Adam and Mary were married in 1788. Their marriage was as happy as John Wesley's was tragic. Thirteen children were born to them, and seven survived to maturity. Mary proved to have the virtues extolled by Peter as the adornment of holy women. "She had a cultivated mind, a sound judgment, and a regenerated heart. She was a worthy companion . . . wise counselor . . . of her grateful husband."[28] She raised a large family and was still ever active as a class leader and visitor of the sick. Adam called her "My beyond all comparison excellent Mary."[29]

Adam was a good father, seeking to find the proper balance between discipline and permissiveness. His children loved and respected him throughout their lives. In his years of extensive travel he frequently took one of the children with him as a traveling companion. Six of his children died; his own namesake, Adam, Jr., died in his arms. His letters at the time of these deaths are most poignant. Many instances, such as the grown children gathering for family communion in the patriarch's home, could be cited to show that this industrious man was also a successful parent.

## A BROADER VIEW OF CLARKE'S WORK

It is to the credit of John Wesley's genius for organization that Methodism did not crumble in confusion after his death in 1791. But it is to the credit of men like Adam Clarke that Wesleyanism continued true to its orthodoxy, committed to evangelism, and pursuing the help of the poor and oppressed. "In the short span of the forty years following the death of John Wesley, England underwent more far-reaching changes than during the whole of the previous two centuries."[30] The Industrial Revolution was hitting its stride, transforming England from a rural, agricultural nation to an urban, industrial one. This gave birth to a new middle class to which Methodism ministered meaningfully while continuing to minister to the lower-class worker. The Methodists were causing a condition of "redemption and lift" in English society. Lower-class persons were converted, shed their "sinful follies," took life seriously, trusted in God, and rose to higher financial and political levels than England's class-conscious society had previously allowed. In a sense, the rise of Adam Clarke to prominence from Irish poverty is an illustration of this movement.

This was the age of the French Revolution, which modeled for the masses of all European nations how to revolt and make it stick. In the literary world the iambs and trochees of the age of Romanticism encouraged revolt against everything. Reform politicians such as Jeremy Bentham, William Cobbett, and Robert Owen were making loud noises about municipal reform, factory acts, poor laws, and slavery.[31] Adam Clarke was calling meetings of Christian textile factory owners to get their support for factory acts to ameliorate sweatshop conditions. Clarke was also leading a Methodist sugar boycott because sugar came largely from slave labor. In Germany rationalistic philosophy and theology and biblical studies were preparing to rock the orthodox Christian world through the works of Hegel, Kant, Bauer, and Strauss.[32]

Miraculously through these times of upheaval, the Methodist Connexion held together with remarkable unity during the 40 years after Wesley's death. This miracle of Methodism may be attributed more to Adam Clarke than to any other person. He had a great deal to do with handing a valid Wesleyan heritage down to the world of the 1830s and beyond.

We have his treasured commentary, and on dust-covered library shelves some of his other works languish. But only 60 sermons remain.[33] Can we discover from those five dozen messages what it was that made Adam Clarke the magnet of multitudes? Why did he receive a royal welcome everywhere he went? A person who had walked miles to hear him preach in Bandon, Ireland, wrote to a friend, "Had a prince entered the town, scarcely greater tokens of respectful recognition could have been shown. Persons were posted all along the street by which the carriages entered from Cork, who had been eagerly awaiting his arrival. Friends and strangers were collected . . . extending thirteen miles, and several had travelled thirty miles to hear the word of life from his lips."[34] "The world knew him as a great scholar, but his own Methodist people knew him also as a prince amongst their preachers."[35]

Can we discover from the 60 sermons what made the Methodist Conference, upon his death, enter into the official minutes, "No man in any age of the church, was ever known, for so long a period, to have attracted larger audiences"?[36]

# 2

# In the Pulpit with Adam Clarke

Delivering, or rather proclaiming, a sermon is not the same as giving a speech about how to make yogurt. The proclaimed word becomes the Word (and not three easy steps to kitchen yogurt) as the preacher's own spirit, soul, and body are poured into the proclamation event which embraces the Holy Spirit, the preacher, and the hearers.

This powerful communication event can be enhanced or negated by the preacher's delivery skills or the lack of same. If the preacher is successful at the preaching moment, all that has gone before—prayer, study, organization of materials, writing, and phrasing—will be free to move men. If, however, the preacher fails at the preaching moment, all that has gone before will be sorely handicapped and even yawned at.

The concerns of delivery *(pronuntiatio)* include: general mode of delivery, appearance, gestures, and voice. We know little about Adam Clarke's delivery from a mere study of his printed sermons. But we can learn a great deal from the writings, journals, and letters of those who heard this great and good man preach.

## CLARKE'S GENERAL METHOD OF PREACHING

### 1. *Extemporaneous*

Clarke preached without notes and without manuscript. Apparently he tried preaching from notes, manuscripts, and from memory when he was very young. But he quickly turned to preaching extemporaneously from the Bible alone. When he did write down something to take with him to the pulpit, it was usually a mere list of scriptures. His clergyman son wrote shortly after his father's death that he had saved a brief outline from which Adam had preached several times. It was a slip of paper 3" x 1" on which Clarke had written a number of Bible references along with the first word of each text.

This mode of preaching was not a labor-saving device. He did not study less because of this informal method. He studied his texts and the subjects, thoroughly developing logical constructs, precise understandings of the words, and mentally noting relationships to everyday life. All the great range of his studies were pursued in light of God's Word and God's call upon his life. His heart and mind were, thus, in constant preparation for the pulpit. His plan of sermon preparation "was to prepare his *mind* rather than his *paper*."[1]

He came to the church concentrating on the sermon. He would seldom visit with anyone before the service but went straight to the "preacher's room" and later came to the pulpit ready to preach.

His extemporaneous method made spontaneity a natural product of his preaching. Most of those who have written about hearing him celebrate his freedom, naturalness, and spontaneity. Mrs. Pawson, the wife of one of Clarke's ministerial colleagues, wrote in a letter:

> Brother Clarke is . . . an extraordinary preacher; and his learning confers great lustre on his talents. He

makes it subservient to grace. His discourses are highly evangelical. . . . *His address is lively, animated, and very encouraging. . . . His words flow spontaneously from the heart;* his views enlarge as he proceeds; he brings to the mind a torrent of things new and old. . . . One can seldom cast an eye on the audience without perceiving a melting unction resting upon them.[2]

As one observer wrote, Clarke's spontaneous preaching allowed him to adjust to the situation and the audience. Thus, "he left the mode of utterance to the warmth of the moment."[3] Clarke gives us his own method of sermon preparation and delivery in a letter to a rookie preacher:

I would lay down two maxims for your conduct: 1. Never *forget* any thing you have learned, especially in language, science, history, chronology, antiquities, and theology. 2. *Improve* in every thing you have learned, and *acquire* what you never had, especially whatever may be useful to you in the work of the ministry.

As to your *making* or *composing* sermons, I have no good opinion of it. Get a thorough knowledge of your subject: understand your text in all its connection and bearings, and then go into the pulpit depending on the Spirit of God to give you power to explain and illustrate to the people those general and particular views which you have already taken of your subject, and which you conscientiously believe to be correct and according to the word of God.

But get nothing by heart to speak there, else even your *memory* will contribute to keep you in perpetual bondage. No man was ever a successful preacher who did not discuss his subject from his own *judgment* and *experience.* The *reciters* of sermons may be popular; but God scarcely ever employs them to convert sinners, or build up saints in their most holy faith.

I do not recommend in this case a blind reliance upon God; taking a text which you do not know how to handle, and depending upon God to give you *something* to say. He will not be thus employed. Go into the pulpit with your understanding full of light, and your heart full of God; and his Spirit will help you, and then you will find a wonderful *assemblage of ideas* coming in to your assistance; and you will feel the benefit of the doctrine of *association,* of which the *reciters* and *memory men* can make no use. The finest, the best, and the most impressive thoughts are obtained in the pulpit when the preacher enters it with the preparation mentioned above.[4]

## 2. *Originality*

Clarke's extemporaneous method resulted in a certain uniqueness, an originality. His son Joseph said he preached as "no other." J. W. Etheridge cites a long list of preaching greats (Chrysostom, Cyprian, Luther, Wesley, Chalmers, Watson, Bunting) and then says that Clarke was not like any of them; "yet was his pulpit ministry distinguished by attributes which set him, in point of effectiveness, on a level with any of them."[5] Clarke studied widely, processed all things through his own mental mill, and what came forth had his own mark upon it.

## 3. *Simplicity*

Clarke did not carry a show of learning into the pulpit. When he was to preach, "He was so completely transformed from the student into the preacher, that he seemed to combine two persons in one, leaving the one in the study and bringing the other to the house of God, full of holy fervour, *simplicity,* and heavenly wisdom. . . . He blended . . . with the wisdom of Solomon, the *simplicity* of a child."[6]

Clarke's hearers usually contrasted his simplicity with the floridly complex pulpit oratory then popular. James Everett, who believed that simplicity was Clarke's greatest perfection, wrote, "Persons who knew him not, might say, he never rose to eloquence."[7] Samuel Dunn added, "He might not in every instance please the admirers of elaborate, artificial eloquence, of studied grace and euphony, of methodical exactness and imaginative brilliancy. . . . The measure of syllables, and the dance of periods were beneath his notice."[8] J. W. Etheridge said, "Clarke's discourses derived no advantage from artificial rhetoric, the mellifluous charms of elocution."[9] Another wrote that he was "perhaps deficient in exquisite taste."[10] One person who heard Clarke preach at Warrington, England, gave this report:

> The orator in the strictest sense was not there, and yet there was an oratory which was the preacher's own. A something which never could have been acquired by art, enchanting to the hearer and peculiar to himself. Some of his etymological criticisms might not meet every mind, but his conceptions were always clear. The *lucidus ordo* was complete and an unction attended the word throughout which was striking and impressive. The whole place, to borrow the language of the upper region, seemed celestialized and the atmosphere itself appeared as though it had undergone a kind of chemical process which enabled the audience to breathe of nothing but heaven.[11]

### 4. *Conviction*

Another quality that characterized Clarke's delivery was conviction. Dunn declared that he brought to the congregation "thoughts that breathe in words that burn."[12] Another observer added, "He had the appearance in the pulpit of one having something to say, and a heart which burned with it, and it found expression in the voice and manner in the readiest and most natural way."[13] "All who heard him," continued J. W. Etheridge, "knew within themselves that they were face to face with a messenger from God."[14] Clarke's son cited the "certainty of his own

[A. Clarke's] mind" and the "convinced feelings of his own heart"[15] as the testimony of conviction which the hearers read and received. "He had a purpose, and one in which you as his hearer, had an everlasting interest. He wanted to make you a better man: he wanted to save your soul; and to do this he sought to lay hold of you by the conscience."[16]

Certainly, artful delivery of lovely cadences can never replace *conviction* in the preacher. Here Clarke coaches us well.

### 5. *Cheerfulness and Compassion*

Clarke's hearers noted an "exhaustless" flow of cheerfulness which it is said added "freshness" to his pulpit ministry, and "awakened a corresponding feeling in his hearers."[17]

His continual preaching on the love and mercy of God and the "earnest affection" with which he called men to salvation and holiness communicated compassion.

## PHYSICAL APPEARANCE

Adam Clarke stood about 5 feet 9 inches tall. As a young man he had a rather muscular build. In old age he was heavyset. His posture was "remarkably erect" even in his later years.

His eyes were small and light gray in color. His complexion was "ruddy"—a healthy reddish color. This complexion made him look younger than he really was, and as a young preacher he was sometimes called "little Adam Clarke." His hair was a "reddish kind of yellow" when he was young. By the time he was 40, however, it was silver gray.

His smile "inspired confidence," and his manner was characterized by kindness, openness, and cheerfulness.

His walk was "buoyant" and his features characteristic of his "benevolence of mind."[18]

Clarke was a neat dresser. He would have nothing to do with the black suits that most of the clergy of the day used. Too drab, he believed, for a preacher of "good news." He generally preached in the attire of an "English country gentleman, with top-boots, drab breeches, blue coat, with covered or silk buttons, pale buff vest, and white neck-cloth."[19]

Joseph, Adam Clarke's preacher son, said there was nothing remarkable about his father's appearance. The most striking thing was his venerable silver hair which he combed back from his forehead.

## Gestures

Some say that Clarke's gestures were few and not remarkably expressive. Yet, Mrs. Pawson (quoted earlier) said his preaching was "lively and animated." But all who remark on his gestures at all agree that they were unstudied, and natural and appropriate to the situation.

In the writing of certain events in Clarke's life we see that gestures were incidentally recorded. Once when he was preaching at Wigan in Lancashire, he paused for an aside in the sermon and said, "Some of you may have seen Adam Clarke before;—more of you may have heard of him;—and among other things, you may have been told that he has studied hard, and read much; but he has to tell you, that he never met with but one book in his life, that he could hug to his heart, and it is this blessed book of God." Then taking up the large Bible that was before him, he placed it to his breast with the endearing embrace of a mother clasping her child to her bosom. The effect was electrical. The simultaneous burst of half-stifled applause was heard through the whole congregation. Men, women,

37

and children were weeping. His own eyes were brimmed with tears. All was simple, natural, touching, sublime.[20] Doubtless the gesture heightened the experience for all.

Preaching on the love of God to man, Clarke offered many "infallible proofs" of God's love. Then in clinching the case, he made a wide, sweeping gesture with his arm as though he were gathering objects. "Then throwing them like alms, in the full bounty of his soul, among the people, 'Here', he said, 'take the arguments among you—make the best of them for your salvation—I will vouch for their solidity—I will stake my credit for intellect on them. Yes, if it were possible to collect them into one, and suspend them, as you would suspend a weight, on a single hair of this gray hair' (here he raised his hand to his silver hair) 'that very hair would be found to be so firmly fastened to the throne of . . . God, that all the devils in hell might be defied to cut it in two!'"[21] Again the congregation was visibly moved "Godward."

Clarke's gestures seem to be called for by the content of the sermon and the situation. This is a good example for us all. As Donald Demaray writes, "Focused behavior fosters attention: irrelevant motion (fumbling, swinging and swaying, nervous shuffling of the feet) causes . . . minds . . . to wander. Human beings are not capable of concentrating when they are confronted by an excess of useless activity."[22] Adam Clarke understood such principles. In his "Letter to a Preacher" he advised about gestures with these wise words:

> Avoid all quaint and fantastic attitudes; all queer noddings, ridiculous stoopings, and erections of your body, skipping from side to side of the desk, knitting your brows; and every other theatrical or foppish air, which tends to disgrace the pulpit, and to render yourself contemptible. Never shake or flourish your handkerchief; this is abominable: nor stuff it into your bosom; this is unseemly. Do not gaze about on

your congregation. Endeavour to gain their attention. Remind them of the presence of God.[23]

Good gestures begin even before the first word of the sermon. Slouching on the platform (a sign of disrespect), scowling at the organist, peering about during prayer, and a nervous approach to the pulpit have nothing to contribute to the success of the sermon. Of Adam Clarke it was said, "He ascends the pulpit as if he felt at home there,"[24] and his manner in the pulpit was that of the calmness of fixed devotion.

## VOICE

Clarke's voice must have been strong—he preached some 15,000 sermons. Thousands of these were preached out of doors. He spoke without a public-address system to throngs numbering up to 10,000 persons. Further, he frequently preached three or four times on Sundays, and while we read of various illnesses, we never hear of a voice problem.

His voice was described as clear, distinct, and full— and at least once as "loud." In 1787, when "little Adam Clarke" had been a preacher for just five years, he received a letter from John Wesley concerning his "long and loud" preaching. On March 13 of that year Adam wrote back:

> As to "loud speaking," I absolutely plead "Not guilty." I think I never did err here from the beginning. I never could see the propriety of *screaming* or *shouting*. I have rather been led to look upon it as a piece of insanity, which in my eyes had not the most remote tendency to accomplish any valuable purpose. I have sometimes exceeded in *length*, but not without self-reprehension, and consequent purposes of amendment; but of this error I am not entirely cured, though I have mended much.[25]

One frequent listener remarked on the "confidence of tone" of Clarke's voice. Another described it as clear and strong, "but not trained in the arts of the elocutionist."[26] Etheridge comments that Clarke's voice was not "tuned at all times to melodious cadences."[27] A close friend said that Clarke had a gift of using a "peculiar elevation of voice" to suddenly accent a climactic moment of impassioned feeling in the sermon. Rev. Joseph Clarke indicated that his father *began* the sermon in a simple, forceful voice; and as the sermon *built* toward the climax, the speaker condenses the strength of the voice, *later* increasing its energy and reaching a *still deeper* current of *fervor* in the conclusion.

Clarke's close friend James Everett admitted, "Persons are to be found with finer voices . . . but without a ray of his genius . . . His voice [was] sufficiently tuned to please; his speaking sufficiently engaging to attract; and his diction, though remote from the ornate, partly through choice, . . . [was] remarkable for its simplicity, its purity, its strength, and its perspicuity."[28]

## THE SUMMING UP

When asked to describe his father's pulpit manner, Rev. Joseph Clarke wrote:

> The appearance of my father, and his effect while in the pulpit upon a stranger, would probably be something like this:
>
> He (the stranger) would see a person of no particular mark, except that time had turned his hair to silver, and the calmness of fixed devotion gave solemnity to his appearance. He spreads his Bible before him, and, opening his hymnbook, reads forth in a clear distinct voice a few verses, after singing of which he offers up a short prayer, which is immediately felt to be addressed to the Majesty of Heaven. The text is proclaimed, and the discourse is begun.
>
> In simple yet forcible language he gives some general information connected with his subject, or lays

down some general positions drawn from either the text or its dependencies. On these he speaks for a short time, fixing the attention by gaining the interest. The understanding feels that it is concerned. A clear and comprehensive exposition gives the hearer to perceive that his attention will be rewarded by an increase of knowledge, or by new views of old truths, or previously unknown uses of ascertained points. He views with some astonishment the perfect collectedness with which knowledge is brought from far, and the natural yet extensive excursions which the preacher makes to present his object in all its bearings, laying heaven and earth, nature and art, science and reason, under contribution to sustain his cause.

Now his interest becomes deeper; for he sees that the minister is beginning to condense his strength, that he is calling in every detached sentence, and that every apparently miscellaneous remark was far from casual, but had its position to maintain, and its work to perform; and he continues to hear with that rooted attention which is created by the importance and clearness of the truths delivered, by the increasing energy of the speaker, and by the assurance in the hearer's own mind that what is spoken is believed to the utmost and felt in its power.

The discourse proceeds with a deeper current of fervor; the action becomes more animated; the certainty of the preacher's own mind, and the feelings of his heart, are shown by the firm confidence of the tone, and a certain fulness of the voice and emphasis of manner; the whole truth of God seems laid open before him; and the soul, thus informed, feels as in the immediate presence of the Lord.[29]

# 3

# What Adam Clarke Preached

If you had been fortunate enough to have strolled into a church in 1520 in Wittenberg, Germany, and heard Martin Luther preach, you would likely have heard a soul-brightening sermon on justification by faith. If you had entered the Old Church in Amsterdam in 1593 to hear Pastor Arminius preach, you would have been treated to an address on free grace. If you had mustered your courage and gone to hear Jonathan Edwards in 1741, you would have been confronted with some variation of "sinners in the hands of an angry God." If you heard Norman Vincent Peale in 1950 or 1980, you probably heard some derivation of the "power of positive thinking." Like all these notables, Adam Clarke was a man of one message. And if you had wedged your way into a Methodist meetinghouse in London, Liverpool, or Dublin, you would have heard that message.

Clarke held his hearers with one great theme. Whenever they crowded out City Road Chapel, Lambeth Chapel, or Stanhope Street Chapel, or rose to hear him preach on the streets at 5 a.m., they knew they would hear some aspect of his one theme. Even if he were the guest speaker called and assigned to raise money for the Lying-in Hospital, Methodist missions, or the Bible Society, the audience could count on him preaching for nearly an hour on his great overarching theme and then taking five minutes at the end of the sermon to raise the money.

Now let's sit Adam Clarke down and ask this great minister to the multitudes what he preached that made people pour into the meeting places at any hour and any place to soak up his sermons. Over the past three years I have read and reread the sermons. I have charted every subject he stressed, rating each one as a "major theme," a "stressed theme," or a "minor theme." Some of the briefer charts will appear in this chapter, and more are found in Appendices 1-4. Let us trace Clarke's theme through his sermons.

I found that Adam Clarke stressed theological or doctrinal subjects over "practics" subjects at a three-to-two ratio. He stressed the great doctrines of the faith six times for each time he stressed social issues. (See Table 1.)

### Table 1

| Comparison of Three Areas of Clarke's Preaching | Major Theme | Stressed Theme | Minor Theme | Raw Score* | Rank |
|---|---|---|---|---|---|
| **Theological Subjects** | 94 | 135 | 49 | 601 | 1 |
| Subjects of Christian Life and Practice | 54 | 96 | 58 | 412 | 2 |
| Subjects of Social Concern | 10 | 22 | 17 | 91 | 3 |

*The "Raw Score" is found by multiplying the number in the "Major Theme" by three, in the "Stressed Theme" by two, and in the "Minor Theme" by one, and then adding the three numbers.

But we need more specific help if we are to ascertain what Clarke's moving messages were about. Table 2 provides a general look at Clarke's theological subjects.

## Table 2

| **Most Stressed General Theological Subjects** | Major Theme | Stressed Theme | Minor Theme | Raw Score | Rank in Theo. Area | Rank in All Categories |
|---|---|---|---|---|---|---|
| Doctrine of Salvation | 47 | 61 | 25 | 288 | 1 | |
| Doctrine of God | 24 | 30 | 9 | 141 | 2 | |
| Doctrines of Man and Sin | 14 | 23 | 5 | 93 | 3 | |
| All Other | 9 | 21 | 10 | 79 | 4 | |
| *Totals* | 94 | 135 | 49 | 601 | | 1 |

## Table 3

| **Most Stressed Specific Theological Subjects** | Major Theme | Stressed Theme | Minor Theme | Raw Score | Rank in Theo. Area |
|---|---|---|---|---|---|
| Sanctification | 17 | 15 | 6 | 87 | 1 |
| Sinfulness of Man | 12 | 13 | 3 | 65 | 2 |
| Atonement | 11 | 14 | 1 | 62 | 3 |
| Love and Grace of God | 14 | 6 | | 54 | 4 |
| Attributes of God | 6 | 14 | 3 | 49 | 5 |
| Salvation by Faith | 5 | 6 | 3 | 30 | 6 |
| Providence | 3 | 7 | 5 | 28 | 7 |
| Christology | 4 | 6 | | 24 | 13 |
| Justification/Pardon | 3 | 6 | 2 | 23 | 8 |
| Revelation (Scriptures) | 3 | 5 | 3 | 22 | 9 |
| Adoption/Repentance/ Regeneration | 4 | 4 | 1 | 21 | 10 |
| Doctrine of Man | 1 | 8 | 1 | 20 | 11 |
| Assurance | 2 | 5. | 3 | 19 | 12 |
| Heaven | 1 | 4 | 5 | 16 | 14 |

44

A more detailed look at Clarke's theological topics shows that holiness was his most stressed subject, followed by the sinfulness of man, the Atonement, and God's gracious love. (See Table 3. Appendix 1 gives a detailed charting of Clarke's theological themes.)

## THEOLOGY IN CLARKE'S SERMONS

There is a typical progression in Clarke's theological sermons. First he establishes by logic, theology, and the Scriptures the greatness, justice, and holiness of God. In the first of his published sermons Clarke follows this pattern. After citing and explaining his text, Jer. 10:11, he logically proves that God is a living, rational essence, most excellent and perfect in wisdom, goodness, and power. He declares, "God . . . is great, good, immaculate and excellent, . . . the most perfect of all Essences . . . we can think of no perfection that he does not possess in an absolute and perfect manner."[1] This he supports with quotations from Thomas Aquinas, Sir Isaac Newton, and John Locke; and to show that even the heathen knew this, he cites Plato.

In another sermon his first main point is "God [is] the cause of all being . . . endowed with various perfections . . . He must be *wise,* and that wisdom infinite. He must be *powerful* and that power infinite. He must be *good* and that goodness unbounded."[2] In other sermons he cites the superlative unity, omnipresence, spirituality, eternity, omniscience, justice, and holiness of God.

After establishing the holy excellencies of God, Clarke typically turns to take a full-color picture of the sinfulness of man in contrast to the perfections of God. Thus, he declares, "A man, looking into his soul, and by the light of God . . . [sees] his sins, more enormous than the tongue can paint them."[3] From scripture, literature, history, and current events Clarke (without being sensational or lurid) catalogs the fact of man's wretched fallenness. "Man is fallen . . . It is vain to dispute against this, there are so many millions of facts to prove it: there is not a man on the face of the earth that is not a proof to it; and the man who rises up to oppose it gives one of the most convincing proofs of it."[4]

Clarke so thoroughly proves the glorious perfection of God and the contrasting wretched sinfulness of man that the hearers must have been at the point of despair. Such was the case of a hardhearted man of "uncommon wickedness" who heard Clarke preach such a sermon from Ps. 37:7-9, affirming the holiness of God and the utter sinfulness of man. Clarke raised his voice and with deep emotion cried, "Who is miserable? Who is athirst? Who is willing to be made happy? Who is willing to be saved?" The wicked man cried aloud, "I am, Lord! I am! I am!"[5] Soon many throughout the congregation were weeping and praying, seeking God.

The next content segment in the sermon progression is Clarke's favorite subject, the doctrine of redemption. He normally begins this part of the sermon by citing the attribute of God which he stresses most—God's love. He declares, "God is loving to every man and hates nothing that he has made."[6] In his sermon "The Love of God to Man" he shows *love* to be the one term that best sums up all the other attributes. He cites his text "God is love" to make the point. Skillfully he touches on various attributes to climax with an accent on God's love.

"I tremble," he says, "before a God of wisdom, because I know he knows me . . . he knows my public haunts and my private ways . . . If I take up his justice, his holiness, or his truth I am similarly circumstanced. From this God of justice what have I a right to expect? . . . [But] because I read he is love . . . I see that God can be just and the justifier of a sinner."[7]

Then Clarke proclaims atonement in Christ. In the sermon just cited, he proceeds to hail the "Savior . . . sent to save us, though sunk low as hell."[8] Clarke cites the atonement through Christ as the monumental evidence of God's love and grace. "As far as sin has reached, so far can God's mercy go," he triumphantly declares.[9] Adam proclaims that salvation not only is graciously offered in Christ, but that it is available only through Christ.

When Clarke addresses the redemption section of the sermon, he stresses two topics: (1) what God has done *for* us: justification by faith; and (2) what God wants to do *in* us: sanctification. Usually, he stresses the latter more. He repeatedly urged his hearers to "be purified by the inspiration of the Holy Spirit,"[10] and to "arise, then, and be baptized with a greater effusion of the Holy Ghost"[11] in order that they might be delivered from all sin.

Thus in the typical theological development of a Clarke sermon we have the picture of a perfect God, the utter sinfulness of man, and the presentation of the gracious atonement of Christ and the full salvation it affords through pardon and purity. Each step is proved by logic and Scripture. Then with "earnest affection" he urges the needy to seek God.

## CHRISTIAN LIFE AND PRACTICE IN CLARKE'S SERMONS

Clarke went to great pains to explain, prove, and convince his hearers of the truth of the great doctrines of God, sin, salvation, and sanctification. But he did not neglect to tell his hearers *what they should do about all this*. Nearly every sermon called for decision and action. He consistently urged the people to make the doctrines of justification and sanctification realities in their lives. Looking back after a half century of preaching Clarke said, "I kept the minds of the people occupied with the doctrines of the cross. I dwelt everywhere upon the importance of a pure heart and its consequent holy conduct."[12] This was his formula—the doctrines of salvation and sanctification fleshed out and made meaningful on Main Street by holy conduct.

He preached on personal discipleship and stressed obedience. Obedience becomes a joy to the sanctified Christian, he affirmed. "When the heart is filled with the love of God and the carnal mind destroyed, then . . . obedience is delightful."[13] "By the finger of God the moral law is written on his heart, and by . . . loving obedience it is transcribed in his life."[14] The Christian is to grow in grace. To his London hearers he declared, "You should have something more today than you had yesterday; if this Sabbath's sun sets without you getting nearer heaven than you were last Sabbath . . . you will not have acted well."[15]

In one-fourth of Clarke's sermons prayer was a major or minor theme. He viewed it as vital to true religion, because "in order to do good a man must receive good; prayer is the way divine assistance is received."[16] Preachers especially he urged to pray, for "a preacher who is not a man of prayer . . . cannot be alive to God in his own soul; nor . . . become instrumental in the salvation of others."[17] He further counsels his hearers, "Those who pray not know nothing . . . of God and know nothing of the state of their soul."[18]

Christian attitudes must be cultivated and expressed. The fruits of the Spirit should be produced, for "even splendid natural abilities adorned with human learning, can be no substitute for the gifts and graces of the Holy Spirit."[19] Peace, joy, love, forgiveness, thanksgiving, hope, and praise were urged by Clarke.

Clarke warned his hearers to avoid backsliding, quarreling, vanity, dishonesty, and worldliness. He urged them to stand firm in trials and temptation, for "whatever evil comes against me is an opposable evil—an evil that can be overcome . . . depend upon it God will . . . make the . . . way out."[20]

Clarke again and again mentions the matter of experimental (experiential) religion and the witness of the Spirit in the life of the Christian, and sometimes it becomes a major theme of a sermon. He describes it as the life of God in the soul of man. It is an assurance not gained from theories, induction or inference, or logical argument. "No human power or cunning can acquire it . . . In this," Clarke declares, "human wit and ingenuity can do nothing. The Spirit himself comes to tell us . . . that we are adopted into the family of heaven."[21] Clarke uses such phrases as mental perception, heart feeling, internal sense, knowing, experience, proving by practical trial, and a spiritual feeling to try to describe the assurance of the Christian.[22] Whatever it is, a man who pretends to religion and has no experiential knowledge of it soon exposes his ignorance, folly, and hypocrisy.[23]

Clarke urges his eager auditors to seek happiness in holy living or they will always be miserable. True "happiness can never be known by any man," he charged, "till sin be expelled from his soul. No holiness, no happiness; and no plenary and permanent happiness without plenary· and permanent holiness."[24]

Tables 4 and 5 show at a glance Clarke's topics on Christian living. See also Appendix 2.

## Table 4

**Rank of General Subjects on Christian Life and Practice**

| | Major Theme | Stressed Theme | Minor Theme | Raw Score | Rank in This Category | Overall Rank |
|---|---|---|---|---|---|---|
| Personal Discipleship | 9 | 24 | 12 | 87 | 1 | |
| Call to Seek God | 4 | 16 | 15 | 59 | 2 | |
| Christian Attitudes | 10 | 7 | 3 | 47 | 3 | |
| Evangelism (Call to Evangelize) | 10 | 5 | 3 | 43 | 4 | |
| The Holy Life | 6 | 10 | | 38 | 5 | |
| Experimental Religion | 7 | 6 | 3 | 36 | 6 | |
| Specific Sins to Avoid | | 11 | 7 | 29 | 7 | |
| Faith and Trust | 5 | 5 | 2 | 27 | 8 | |
| Stewardship | | 9 | 3 | 21 | 9 | |
| Christian Service | 3 | 3 | | 15 | 10 | |
| *Totals* | 54 | 96 | 48 | 402 | | 2 |

## Table 5

**Top-ranking Particular Topics on Christian Life and Practice**

| | Major Theme | Stressed Theme | Minor Theme | Raw Score | Rank |
|---|---|---|---|---|---|
| Evangelistic Appeal | 4 | 16 | 15 | 59 | 1 |
| Holy Living | 5 | 8 | | 31 | 2 |
| Missions | 8 | 1 | 2 | 28 | 3 |
| Prayer | 1 | 9 | 6 | 27 | 4 |
| Growth, Discipline, Obedience | 3 | 5 | 1 | 20 | 5-6-7 |
| Temptation/Trials | 3 | 5 | 1 | 20 | 5-6-7 |
| Religious Experience | 4 | 3 | 2 | 20 | 5-6-7 |
| Faith/Trust | 4 | 3 | 1 | 19 | 8 |
| Money | | 8 | 1 | 17 | 9 |
| Christian Service | 3 | 3 | | 15 | 10 |
| Perseverance | 2 | 3 | | 12 | 11 |
| Peace/Joy | 2 | 2 | 1 | 11 | 12 |

# Social Concerns

As Table 1 clearly shows, Clarke's preaching stressed the great Christian doctrines and the Christian life about 10 times more than the social concerns of the day. This does not mean that he was not interested in such, as we shall see in a later chapter. He was deeply involved in social causes, but he did not bring them to the pulpit with great vigor. Remember, he preached during the era of the American Revolution, the French Revolution, and the Napoleonic Wars. He advised that politics not take over the pulpits.

Clearly the most eminent social cause upon which he preached was helping the poor, for which the Methodists were famous. Table 6 charts the social concerns Clarke preached on.

## Table 6

**Topics of Social Concerns in Clarke's Preaching**

| | Major Theme | Stressed Theme | Minor Theme | Raw Score | Rank |
|---|---|---|---|---|---|
| Helping the Poor | 6 | 9 | 2 | 38 | 1 |
| Slavery/Prejudice, etc. | | 5 | 1 | 11 | 2 |
| Business Ethics | 1 | 1 | 5 | 10 | 3 |
| Education | 1 | 2 | 2 | 9 | 4 |
| Political Corruption | | 3 | 1 | 7 | 5-6 |
| Poverty and Riches, etc. | 1 | 2 | | 7 | 5-6 |
| Good Citizenship | 1 | | 2 | 5 | 7 |
| Church and State | | | 2 | 2 | 8-9 |
| War | | | 2 | 2 | 8-9 |

It should be noted that the themes cited in this chapter do not record every topic mentioned by Clarke, but only those treated strongly enough to be counted as "major," "stressed," or "minor" themes.

Considering all the specific themes from all categories formed in the 60 sermons, we make the discoveries shown in Table 7.

## Table 7

| Most Stressed Specific Subjects Considering All Categories | Major Theme | Stressed Theme | Minor Theme | Raw Score | Rank |
|---|---|---|---|---|---|
| Sanctification | 17 | 15 | 6 | 87 | 1 |
| Sinfulness of Man | 12 | 13 | 3 | 65 | 2 |
| Atonement | 11 | 14 | 1 | 62 | 3 |
| Call to Seek God | 4 | 16 | 15 | 59 | 4 |
| Love and Grace of God | 14 | 6 | | 54 | 5 |
| Attributes of God | 6 | 14 | 3 | 49 | 6 |
| Helping the Poor | 6 | 9 | 2 | 38 | 7 |
| The Holy Life | 5 | 8 | | 31 | 8 |
| Salvation by Faith | 5 | 6 | 3 | 30 | 9 |
| Providence | 3 | 7 | 5 | 28 | 10-11 |
| Missions | 8 | 1 | 2 | 28 | 10-11 |
| Prayer | 1 | 9 | 6 | 27 | 12 |
| Justification/Pardon | 3 | 6 | 2 | 23 | 13 |
| Revelation (Bible) | 3 | 5 | 3 | 22 | 14 |
| Adoption/Regeneration | 4 | 4 | 1 | 21 | 15 |

From this journey through Clarke's major topics we come now to the task of reducing 60 sermons comprising 1,600 pages, 512,000 words, to one syllogism. This is not difficult—the syllogism would go something like this:

God is infinitely holy.

We are hopelessly sinful, but

God graciously offers *full salvation* through Christ by faith to which His Spirit witnesses.

We must then *seek, find,* and *live* this full salvation.

This brings us closer to Adam Clarke's one message: *Full salvation now by grace through faith.*

What the people poured in to hear was the *kerygma*—not fads or trivialities or pop psychology. It was the gospel they wanted, needed, and received.

# 4

# On Whose Authority?

The only sources quoted in a sermon I heard recently were a local sportswriter, the Mary Worth comic strip, and the preacher's mother-in-law. Oh, the preacher tipped his hat to two lines from the Psalms—out of habit, I guess, for he never returned to the Scripture. My response to his cute conclusion was, So what? Who says besides the sports page, Mary Worth, and your mother-in-law?

In validating the concepts, content, and conclusions of any preacher, the authorities he calls upon to testify for his case must be evaluated. A preacher may sprinkle his sermon with soap-opera stories, or he may saturate it with Scripture. In this chapter we shall explore and evaluate the sources of Adam Clarke and the way these sources are used.

## ADAM CLARKE AND THE BIBLE

Clarke anchored every sermon on the Gibraltar of Holy Scripture. He loved the Bible, gave his life to its study, and preached it with carefulness and power.

In a letter to a friend Adam Clarke wrote, "I have lived more than three score years and ten; I have traveled a good deal, by sea and by land; I have conversed with and seen many people, in and from many different countries; I have studied all the principal religious systems in the world; I have read much, thought much, and reasoned much; and the result is, I am persuaded of the simple, unadulterated truth of no *book but the Bible;* and of the excellence of no system of religion but that contained in the holy scriptures! And especially Christianity, which is referred to in the Old Testament and fully revealed in the New."[1]

Clarke believed that if God had given him any gift, it was the gift of explaining the Scriptures. He became the Bible teacher of Methodism; and how carefully he went about it. As a sort of warmup exercise before beginning his commentary, he translated the entire Bible, comparing every word and variant reading with the dozens of Greek, Hebrew, Latin, and Arabic manuscripts which he owned and with other manuscripts available in the libraries of the land. He worked on the commentary for some 30 years. Studying, teaching, and preaching the Bible was his life.

Clarke declared that the Bible should form the creed. Too many creed builders, he told his hearers in Lerwick, make their creeds first, building them according to their own biases, and then hunt up passages in the Bible "dismembered from their fellows"[2] to give a biblical ring to their homemade creed.

In speaking of the New Testament canon, he urged his people to view these writings as "the pure sayings of the Holy Ghost"[3] whose promises and judgments will be infallibly fulfilled. This was not an expression of a verbal inspiration theory, for Clarke says in introducing the New Testament part of his commentary that his doctrine was

55

"not for such an inspiration as implies that even the words were dictated or their phrases suggested to them by the Holy Ghost. . . . They were *hagiographers,* who are supposed to be left to the use of their own words."[4] He described inspiration in terms of *suggestion, direction,* and the "broad seal" of the Holy Spirit.[5]

After citing several special ways of inspiration, Clarke says that the most common way was by "direct inspiration; by the powerful agency of God on the mind, giving it a strong conception and supernatural persuasion of the truth . . . without any mixture of error. . . . We must ever consider these Scriptures as coming from God, as divinely inspired, and as containing his infallible truth."[6]

Clarke believed that much was to be gained by close study of the variant readings in the old manuscripts; for in the preprinting era when so much hand copying of manuscripts was being done, "great ignorance prevailed both in literature and religion, it was not likely that the best helps, even had they been at hand, would have been critically used; therefore, those primitive editions must necessarily have been . . . imperfect . . . as scribes would alter or amend from conjecture where they did not have access to the original manuscripts."[7] Thus he felt free in his sermons both to praise and correct the King James Version.

He further believed that critical word study was profitable because "to quote and analyze the original words . . . has given us an extension and force of meaning which we could not have otherwise acquired."[8]

Historical study was vital to Clarke. In three of his recorded sermons he tells the people that the Epistles can be properly understood only when we know the "circumstances of the writers, and the state of the people to whom the letters were addressed."[9]

Clarke opposed both the flamboyant allegorizing and the wooden literalism of his day which treated the Bible as a book of magic on the one hand and a code of proof texts on the other. He fathered a reverent sort of biblical criticism. He probably would not want to claim either the title of "critic" or all of his alleged critical offspring, for he was sure that through his own critical efforts "infidelity can expect no help; false doctrine no support; and even true religion no accessions to its excellence; though a few beams may be thus added to its lustre."[10]

Regarding certain critics who felt obligated to denature the Gospels, Clarke wrote, "I have read my Bible as closely as any of them, perhaps as any 10 or 20 of them, I have weighed its every syllable, sentence by sentence, and word by word"; and he added that the Gospel writers said nothing that Jesus' "own words and conduct did not authorize them to say."[11]

Believing that "without an interpreter the things recorded in God's Book are incapable of all the purposes of salvation"[12] Clarke believed that every preacher should be an ardent student of the Word. As noted, he urged many, including a younger colleague, to "study yourself half to death and then pray yourself wholly to life."[13] He believed that the study of the Bible was a lifelong challenge; during his 71st year he read the Bible through again from the oldest manuscripts.

It is no wonder that a man so saturated in the Bible should preach sermons saturated with the Bible. To preach the Bible was a grave responsibility. "He never entered the pulpit but . . . with a painful sensation of his responsibility as a messenger of the Gospel. . . . The thought of inadequately declaring the counsels of God as to make the Gospel of none effect," wrote his son, "frequently drank up his spirit and made his soul tremble."[14]

# How Adam Clarke Used the Bible in His Sermons

## 1. *Exposition*

To Clarke, the Bible was a revelation of God's nature, work, and will. It was then the great source to be explained, unraveled, and applied. Thus most of his sermons were basically expository.

Actual phrases or clauses from the text frequently formed the main points or subpoints of his sermons. Clarke's sermons were, however, far more than running comments on the scripture, a practice that so frequently masquerades as expository preaching. Rather he marshalled the teachings of the text into a logical, step-by-step development toward a powerful conclusion.

An example of his expository work is found in his sermon on Ps. 15:1-5:

> Lord, who shall abide in thy tabernacle? who shall dwell in thy holy hill? He that walketh uprightly, and worketh righteousness, and speaketh the truth in his heart. He that backbiteth not with his tongue, nor doeth evil to his neighbour, nor taketh up a reproach against his neighbour. In whose eyes a vile person is contemned; but he honoureth them that fear the Lord. He that sweareth to his own hurt, and changeth not. He that putteth not out his money to usury, nor taketh reward against the innocent. He that doeth these things shall never be moved.

In expositing the meaning of the passage, he derives two important questions which need to be answered.

1. Who can be considered a worthy member of the Church Militant upon the earth?

2. Who, after life is ended, shall be received into heaven?

Bringing the New Testament to bear on the Old Testament text (a good habit for preachers), Clarke declares the answer to these questions to be the person who has been "freely justified through the redemption that is in Jesus; and has had . . . his heart cleansed by the inspiration of God's Holy Spirit [and has] the eleven moral excellencies"[15] of the text ("worketh righteousness, . . . speaketh the truth," etc.).

The "eleven moral excellencies" made up the exposition of the text, coming directly from it and being supported by 15 word studies, 8 quotations from and allusions to the Old Testament, and 12 quotations from and allusions to the New Testament. Also seven versions or old manuscripts were cited along with three rabbinical sources, three church creeds noted and quoted, one modern churchman quoted, and two classical authors cited. There were four poetic quotations (Chaucer and Herbert) and two common proverbs of the day were also brought in to support the teaching of the text. After this evidence, testimony, and proof Clarke closed the sermon with this appeal: "Go now to Christ, that he may purge your conscience from dead works, baptize you with the spirit of holiness, guide you by his counsel, and at last—receive you into his glory."[16]

## 2. Choice of Texts

The whole Bible provided preaching material for Clarke. The 60 published sermons have texts selected from 29 different books. Clarke frequently preached on the text of the day in the Anglican lectionary. If the published sermons truly represent Clarke's text selection, we see that he chose New Testament texts 70 percent of the time. (Table 1 charts Clarke's text selection.)

# TABLE 1

**Source of Texts of Clarke's Published Sermons**

| A. *New Testament* | *Number of Texts* |
|---|---|
| 1. Pauline Epistles | 18 |
| 2. Synoptic Gospels | 9 |
| 3. Johannine Writings | 6 |
| 4. General Epistles | 5 |
| 5. Hebrews | 3 |
| 6. Acts | 3 |
| *Total* | 44 |
| B. *Old Testament* | |
| 1. Wisdom Literature | 9 |
| 2. The Prophets | 6 |
| 3. Historical Books | 2 |
| 4. Pentateuch | 1 |
| *Total* | 18 |
| *Grand Total* | 62* |

*Two of the 60 sermons had dual texts.

When Clarke selected a text, he did not merely lightly nod to it on the way to making some other point—he preached it. He quoted the text or a part of it an average of 11 times per sermon.

Since he was a preacher of "full salvation now by grace through faith," it is not surprising that Clarke found more texts from the writings of Paul than from any other Bible writer.

## 3. *Bible Quotations and Allusions*

Besides quoting his text 11 times per sermon, Clarke quoted, on the average, 15 other passages of scripture during each sermon. Thus the biblical authority rang loud and clear with 26 Bible quotations per sermon. In addition he used 9 or 10 biblical allusions per sermon. In this manner the truth was buttressed with 35 or 36 (35.34 to be exact) quotations from or allusions to the Bible. (See Appendices 3 and 4 for a detailed charting of Clarke's use of quotations and allusions.) Table 2 gives an overview of Clarke's use of the Bible.

## TABLE 2

### Clarke's Quotations from the Bible

A. *Most Quoted Biblical Writers*

| | | |
|---|---|---|
| 1. Paul | 384 quotations |
| 2. John | 170 quotations |
| 3. Psalmists | 158 quotations |
| 4. Matthew | 114 quotations |

B. *Most Often Quoted Books*

| | |
|---|---|
| 1. Psalms | 158 |
| 2. Matthew | 114 |
| 3. John | 93 |
| 4. Acts (41 in one sermon) | 91 |
| 5. 1 & 2 Corinthians | 85 |
| 6. 1 & 2 Peter | 77 |
| 7. Romans | 70 |
| 8. Genesis | 66 |

C. *Sections of the Bible Ranked in Order of Times Quoted*

| | |
|---|---|
| 1. Pauline Epistles | 384 |
| 2. Wisdom Literature | 250 |
| 3. Synoptic Gospels | 217 |
| 4. Johannine Literature | 170 |
| 5. Hebrews and General Epistles | 151 |
| 6. Pentateuch | 125 |
| 7. Prophets | 121 |
| 8. Acts | 91 |
| 9. Historical Books, Old Testament | 46 |

D. *Summaries*
  1. Total biblical quotations in the
     60 sermons                                1,555
  2. Average number of quotations per section   25.9
  3. Average number of references to the text
     per sermon                                 10.9
  4. Average number of biblical allusions
     per sermon                                  9.3
  5. Average number of quotations and
     allusions per sermon                       35.34

## 4. *Word Studies*

Most of the preachers the Methodists heard in Clarke's day were not highly educated. Therefore, Greek and Hebrew word studies were rare and apparently welcome. Clarke's sermons average 12 word studies per sermon. It should be pointed out that the 41 sermons Clarke edited for publication averaged 16.5 word studies per sermon, while the ones taken down in shorthand by an anonymous listener contain only 1.42 word studies per sermon. Two things impinge here: (1) The shorthand taker admitted that he did not get everything, but managed to take down the heart of the sermon. Would the references to Greek and Hebrew be what the auditor might by necessity leave out? (2) Clarke never prepared a manuscript or even an outline before preaching. When, therefore, by popular demand he went to the study to reconstruct the sermon after the fact for publication, he included more word studies (and other elements) in light of the permanency of the written word, and in light of a different audience. Whatever the case, word studies were an important part of his use of the Bible. He also brought in word study from other languages. It is said he knew 20 languages; he used word studies from 12 in the 60 sermons being studied here.

## TABLE 3

**Citing of Original Scriptural Language and Other Word Studies**

| | 41 Edited Sermons | Average per Sermon | 19 Unedited Sermons | Average per Sermon | Total All 60 Sermons | Average per Sermon |
|---|---|---|---|---|---|---|
| Greek or Hebrew | 597 | 14.56 | 26 | 1.36 | 623 | 10.38 |
| Anglo-Saxon | 20 | .48 | | | 20 | |
| Latin | 46 | 1.12 | 1 | .05 | 47 | |
| French | 6 | .146 | | | 6 | |
| German | 2 | .04 | | | 2 | |
| Arabic | 2 | .04 | | | 2 | |
| Ethiopic | 1 | .02 | | | 1 | |
| Danish | 1 | .02 | | | 1 | |
| Dutch | 1 | .02 | | | 1 | |
| Gothic | 1 | .02 | | | 1 | |
| Teutonic | 1 | .02 | | | 1 | |
| Totals | 678 | 16.51 | 27 | 1.42 | 705 | 11.75 |

Clarke's use of the original languages was not to parade his learning, but to make the Bible live. Here is an example of how Clarke used word studies. When preaching from the Lord's Prayer, Clarke, in defining prayer, cites the phrase "When thou prayest" and then cites the original language with these words:

> When thou prayest, οταν προσευχη . The word προσευχη, prayer, is compounded of προς, to or with, and ευχη, a vow; because, to pray aright, a man binds himself to God as by a vow, to live to his glory, if he will grant him his grace. The verb ευχομαι signifies to pour out prayers or vows, from ευ, well, and χεω, I pour out, probably alluding to the offerings or libations which were poured out before or on the altar. As in ancient times prayers were scarcely ever offered to the Divine Being without sacrifice or oblation, hence the reason the word which is used to express prayer. Sacri-

63

fice was therefore understood to be essentially necessary to prayer.[17]

## 5. *Various Versions and Manuscripts*

The *New International Version,* the *New American Standard Bible,* the *Revised Standard Version,* and so forth, were not at the tip of Clarke's fingers, yet he cited many versions and manuscripts, many of which he owned. Seventy-nine times in the 60 sermons he calls another version or translation to testify, in order to clarify the truth. He cites the Massoretic text, the Septuagint, Syriac, the Samaritan Bible, the Arabic, the Vulgate, besides the Wycliffe, Coverdale, and other more recent translations of his day.

## 6. *Illustrations*

We will deal later with Clarke's art of sermon illustration (or the lack of it). Let it suffice at this point to say that 20 percent of his sermon illustrations were biblical examples.

In all of the preceding ways Clarke used the Bible as the primary source of authority, the one rule of faith and practice. It was the final court of appeal, the irrefutable proof, the anchored authority. To bring clear biblical proof to a human problem or debate was, for Clarke, to settle the issue. If human reason, weakness, whims, or practice ran against biblical teaching, Clarke's answer was "God requires whatever his word requires. He will not bring down the moral law to our weakness and fall; but he will bring us up to it."[18]

Thus we see Adam Clarke a "man of one book" in the Wesleyan sense. Is it not accurate to say that part of being true to the Wesleyan heritage is to saturate our souls and our sermons with the Bible?

# EXTRABIBLICAL SOURCES QUOTED IN CLARKE'S SERMONS

The quality of the "authorities" one brings to testify for the truth is an important measure of the speaker's *"invention."* Whom you quote does make a difference. I heard two sermons on prayer about one month apart. One made me want to pray, the other seemed frothy as whipped cream. While a number of factors contributed to the character of the sermons, one important difference was that one quoted a baseball player, a Hollywood actress, and his own book on prayer; while the other quoted Teresa, Thomas a Kempis, and Frank Laubach.

Adam Clarke made his quotes count. Clarke used 329 extrabiblical quotations in the 60 sermons, an average of 5 to 6 quotations per sermon. In the 60 sermons he quoted the ancient Greek and Latin classics 67 times. Of course these were not Christian authors, but these classics have lived on for good reason. The ancient Greeks and Romans have been the world's teachers in literature, drama, logic, and philosophy. Further, when Clarke cited these writers, he was citing authors and works who made up a great percentage of the grammar school experience of the Britishers who heard him preach. All those in the audience who had gone to school at all had done battle with Vergil, Cicero, Plato, and Socrates.

One area which Clarke knew, as few others of his day, was the ancient rabbinical, Persian, and Arabic writings. These he studied with great care and quoted from them 40 times in the published sermons.

Clarke also knew the history of Christianity very well. He quoted the Church fathers 22 times, the medieval and Reformation churchmen 14 times. He knew his contemporary religious scene and quoted contemporary churchmen

# TABLE 4

**Extrabiblical Sources Cited in Clarke's Sermons**

| | Number of Different Authors | Number of Quotations | Average Number Per Sermon | Typical Sources |
|---|---|---|---|---|
| Ancient Classical Authors | 36 | 67 | 1.11 | Cicero, Plato, Aristotle, Horace, Vergil |
| Rabbinical, Persian, Arabic Writings | 15 (est.) | 40 | .66 | Ben Ezra, Chaldean Targums, Talmud |
| Church Fathers | 15 | 22 | .36 | Augustine, Origen, Tertullian, Athanasius, Chrysostom |
| Medieval, Pre-Reformation Churchmen | 5 | 7 | .116 | Aquinas |
| Reformers | 4 | 7 | .116 | Luther, Calvin |
| Old European Literature | 9 | 24 | .40 | Milton, Shakespeare, Chaucer, Spenser |
| Contemporary Churchmen | 31 | 50 | .83 | John Wesley, Wakefield, Newton, Calmet, Kaimes, Horne |
| Contemporary Literature | 26 | 39 | .65 | Locke, Hooker, Paley, Leigh, Addison |
| Liturgies and Creeds | 4 | 21 | .35 | Westminster Catechism |
| Common Proverbs | 6 | 9 | .15 | |
| Unidentified Quotes | 10 (est.) | 43 | .71 | |
| *Totals* | 161 | 329 | 5.48 | |

50 times. He quoted the man he admired most—John Wesley—but cited 30 other contemporaries as well.

Realizing that he needed to relate his messages to the religious background of his hearers, he cited 21 times the liturgies and creeds in which many of his hearers had been catechized. He also quoted nine common proverbs of the times which were, of course, the common wisdom of the people who heard him.

Like Wesley, Clarke "preached plain truth to plain people." He deliberately avoided ornate language. Nevertheless, he sometimes gave his sermons a certain grace by quoting the best English literature. Adding beauty to a sermon on the Jewish sacrificial system, he cites a stanza from Fletcher's "Purple Island" which ends:

*Eyes' light, heart's love, soul's only life He is;*
*Life, soul, love, heart, light, eye, and all, are His:*
*His eye, light, heart, love, soul; He all my joy and bliss.*

From Milton, who seems to be his favorite, he points to the hopelessness of sin (before hoisting the hope of the gospel) by citing Satan's hopelessness in *Paradise Lost:*

*So farewell hope, and with hope farewell fear,*
*Farewell remorse; all good to me is lost;*
*Evil, be thou my good.*

Clarke quoted, or alluded to, the Bible seven times for every time he quoted any other source (compare tables 2 and 4 and Appendix 4). Table 4 depicts the particulars about Clarke's quoting from extrabiblical sources.

The foregoing survey of Clarke's use of the Bible leaves no wonder about why his preaching rang with more authority than any drill sergeant ever dared to dream of. First, Clarke invoked the authority of the Word of God. Then this was buttressed with quotations and illustrations from the best of the theologians, philosophers, poets, historians, linguists, writers, scientists, and statesmen. And that's a lot better than Mary Worth or even your mother-in-law.

# 5

# Logic Is a Preacher's Best Friend

Truth *proved* beyond any reasonable doubt is not just the chum of the trial lawyer, it is also a fast friend of the Christian preacher. Today this faithful friend needs to be given an engraved invitation to enter our sermons, stretch his legs, and make himself at home. He should be allowed to roam at will through our homiletic introductions and main divisions. And he should permanently inhabit our conclusions.

"Much of what has passed for evangelical preaching has been intellectually weak," says Roy Short, "and frequently untenable ideas have been uttered with such vehemence and dogmatism as to provoke thinking people to disgust."[1] Apollos "mightily convinced the Jews" (Acts 18:28) with logical scriptural argument, and Paul saw his task as persuading men (2 Cor. 5:11), knowing that only sound doctrinal argument can convince some people (Titus 1:9). For a lesson in logical argument in preaching, analyze the sermons of such men as Charles Spurgeon, Reuben A. Torrey, John Wesley, and Adam Clarke.

Clarke did not depend on deathbed stories, emotional tales, or flamboyant rhetoric to carry the impact of the sermon. Rather he depended on the force of content, the power of proven truth. His sermons so proved the logic, wisdom, and necessity of turning to God *now* that the resister was left without defense. The typical Clarke sermon proved the holiness and justice of God, the wretched sinfulness of man, the truth of atonement by grace through Christ, and the reasonableness and urgency of seeking pardon or purity *now*.

Adam Clarke realized the same truth echoed by Robert L. Sumner: "Power in the pulpit will be determined by the degree in which you offer proof of your contentions."[2] By the time Clarke had amassed overwhelming arguments for God's holiness, man's sinfulness, and God's gracious offer of redemption, many people would be quietly weeping, some would be praying aloud, and on some occasions when the skillful closure of argument came together, the people burst into spontaneous applause.

Some of Clarke's critics falsely accused him of rationalism. Others said that sometimes his long, involved arguments were hard to follow. Doubtless this is one of the hazards of logical preaching. But it is definitely superior to the hodgepodge sermon that is developed by simply picking a subject, consulting the concordance, and stringing together random, jumbled comments on every verse listed. Every one of Clarke's published sermons can be reduced to a syllogism and then to a one-sentence thesis or proposition.

## THE LOGICAL DEVELOPMENT OF WHOLE SERMONS

Let us look at "The Necessity of Christ's Atonement," a sermon preached by Clarke at City Road Chapel, London, on April 30, 1820, the Missionary Anniversary. This sermon was taken down in shorthand and published after Clarke's death with no note of divisions of main points or subheads. Yet the progression is easy to follow because of the flow of logic.

The thesis of the sermon is: In accordance with God's will Jesus died for all men; we must therefore preach this word to all men everywhere.

Reduced to a categorical syllogism, it is:

Through Scripture, logic, history, experience, and theology we know that Christ died for the sins of all men and women, according to the will of God.

We are men and women for whom Christ died.

We are therefore indebted to Him to carry His message of salvation to all men everywhere by supporting world missions.

The text for the sermon is Luke 24:46-48.

And [Jesus] said unto them, Thus it is written, and thus it behoved Christ to suffer, and to rise from the dead the third day: and that repentance and remission of sins should be preached in his name among all nations, beginning at Jerusalem. And ye are witnesses of these things.

The logical development proceeds in this manner. The point to be proved is that "divine grace, the incarnation, and passion, and death, and burial, and resurrection of Him who is the Author of this gospel" is the *valid* Good News to man. Clarke takes up the task of proving this beyond any reasonable doubt:

1. *Logical validation.* Clarke briefly opposes certain objections to the Atonement.

2. *Historical validation.* Clarke cites the Law of the prophets, Jesus, the Church fathers, the saints, and the Church.

3. *Experiential validation.* Here the preacher proclaims that if he had no other proof of the Atonement

71

than the experience and testimony of those who had been "partakers . . . of the pardon of sin . . . (and) the sanctifying influences of . . . the Holy Spirit" that it would "content my mind upon the subject."[3]

4. *Scriptural validation.* Clarke proceeds, citing 10 New Testament passages and 6 Old Testament passages.

5. *Theological validation.* Clarke resorts to an examination of the nature of God to show that it is natural to expect redeeming action from such a Being.

After this extensive validation (3,000 words) Clarke summarizes his argument in a 400-word statement, declaring, "Now I know not a flaw in this argument; I believe there is not a man under heaven who can find one. The thing is determined forever."[4]

Clarke then moves to an exposition of the text, stressing these points on the authority of the proven Atonement in Christ alone:

1. Repentance is to be proclaimed, v. 47a.
2. Remission of sins is to be proclaimed, v. 47a.
3. These proclamations are to be to all nations, v. 47c.
4. We are indebted to Him to carry the message to men and women everywhere.
5. We can do this by giving money and ourselves to the cause of Methodist missions.

In his sermon "Salvation by Faith" Clarke uses proofs from the same five categories (Scripture, logic, experience, history, theology) to show that justification and sanctification can only come by faith. This he establishes after refuting salvation by works, suffering, reincarnation, and God's general benevolence.

## INTERNAL USE OF LOGIC

The overall arc made by Clarke's whole sermon was logical. The hounds of deduction and induction were whistled for to make sure the traits of the *subpoints* were logical as well.

Sometimes the very language of the sermon was syllogistic. Here is an example from "The Rich Man and the Beggar":

> The final separation of an unholy soul from God, is a necessary consequence of the state in which it is found. For as it is unholy, it cannot be united to God, because God is holy. If then it cannot be united to him, it must be separated from him; and as he is the fountain of happiness, to be separated from him is to be separated from happiness and consequently to be in . . . misery.[5]

This thought illustrates deductive logic and may be expressed in this *disjunctive* syllogism:

> Unholy persons will either be united with God in happiness or separated from God in misery.
> They will be separated from Him in misery.
> Therefore they will not be united with God in happiness.

Again it could be expressed as a logical *dilemma:*

> If sinful persons remain unholy, they will be miserable in this life and separated from God in the next.
> Both present misery and eternal separation from God are intolerable.
> Sinful persons, therefore, must not remain unholy.

In preaching on "The Doctrine of Holiness," Clarke declares:

> Having transgressed God's law, it proves there is in us an evil principle, which has led us to transgress; for the transgression of the law in the life is only the external manifestation of what is in the heart; and as man acts from inward feelings, an unrighteous act sufficiently ascertains an unrighteous principle.[6]

An analysis of the logic here results in a valid *categorical* syllogism:

What is within the person's heart is expressed in his behavior.

All persons express sin and evil.

Therefore, the human heart is evil.

In another sermon Clarke argues:

> There are no limits in the Divine Being; for whatever is an attribute of God, must be as extensive as the nature of which it is an attribute; otherwise, this would argue imperfection in the Divine Being. We argue, then, that if grace be an attribute of God, it must necessarily be infinite and eternal.[7]

This brief argument, and the further implications made by Clarke, springs from this *categorical* syllogism:

The attributes of God are infinite, perfect, eternal, and unlimited.

Grace is an attribute of God.

Therefore, God's grace is infinite, perfect, eternal, and unlimited.

Clarke goes on to show his listeners in City Road Chapel, London, on June 11, 1816, that since he has proved that God's grace is infinite, perfect, eternal, and unlimited that not one of them, regardless of how deep in sin they might be, were beyond the reach of such grace.

## CLARKE'S INDUCTIVE REASONING

Clarke used *induction* freely. He generalized from specific cases, cited cause and effect, argued from criteria, used illustrations and metaphors which argue from similarities as does this inductive analogy which comes from Clarke's citing the requirements laid upon the runners in the early Olympics: "Can you suppose, then, if moral honesty, strictness, attention, uprightness, and truth . . . is so essentially necessary to running, wrestling, or boxing, that God will take to heaven . . . any man impure and unholy?"[8]

Illustrations are a form of inductive reasoning when they are used as *specific* examples to prove the *general* point the preacher is making. Adam Clarke used illustrations in this way.

Like Wesley, Adam Clarke was not a master of sermon illustration. Although he used six or seven illustrations per each hour-long sermon, the illustrations were usually very brief. A two- or three-sentence example would do for him. He almost never depended on illustrations to provide the major emotional impact of the sermon; this would come from content and forceful logical argument which his illustrations were meant to augment. His illustrations were never embellishments of tear-jerking incidents.

Clarke's illustrations sometimes lacked specific detail. This could be considered a defect. For example, in preaching from Isa. 1:18, "Come now, and let us reason together, saith the Lord: though your sins be as scarlet, they shall be white as snow," he uses this illustration:

> We know that we are in possession of methods of fixing tints, making stains and fixing them; but we know we can find out no method of discharging these stains. It is very rarely, if not entirely, impossible to take out any tint from any substance, without less or more destroying the fibre, or texture of the thing submitted to the process. It is God alone that can discharge the stain of sin from the soul.[9]

Could this not have been improved by using a specific incident—beet juice spilled on a Sunday shirt, a printer's ink accident, bleaching a hole in a blouse trying to remove spaghetti sauce, etc.? We know that the specific illustration makes greater impact than the general.

Adam Clarke used some 387 illustrations in the 60 sermons. His main source of illustrations was *common life experiences.* Links in a chain are used to depict the relationship of certain theological truths: ruling the soul is compared to government of the state; payment of employees or servants is used to show certain aspects of the God-man relationship. The life of Mr. Gilpin is used to demonstrate God's providence. The artist's ability to recognize his own painting amidst other works of art explains how God recognizes His own; the precision and care of embroidery work is compared to God's careful work in the heart of the Christian; and a man with no money, bread, or job is used to depict the sinner who must come to God for salvation by grace alone.

Wisely, Clarke picked many illustrations from the world of *health and science*. Health matters still seem to fascinate people—prayer request lists and soap operas are both dominated by health problems. Clarke illustrates sin by describing it as an imbibed poison; he compares the human heart sending blood throughout the body to how London should send Bibles, money, and missionaries throughout the world; he compares leprosy and sin; he describes the process of nutrition and death; and he illustrates spiritual health by describing physical health. He also uses the sciences of mineralogy, astronomy, and geology to explain spiritual truth.

Clarke was a man who loved the out-of-doors; thus 42 of his illustrations come from the *realm of nature*. He cites the hopes of a deer hunter to illustrate the meaning of a scripture phrase. "Fishes live not on the elms, and cattle browse not in the depths of the sea," he observes and then goes on to show that "hell is for demons . . . heaven, for holy angels, and the spirits of just men made perfect."[10] Thunder, lightning, rain, snow, the planets, the sun, the grass, evaporation, soil, wells, oysters, and even camel's milk are recruited to communicate spiritual truth.

*Ancient history and ancient customs* provided Clarke with some of his most enlightening illustrations. He explained how part of Psalm 19 is illuminated by understanding the ancient Hebrew marriage ceremony and customs. The Lord's Prayer he makes more plain by citing a custom of ancient Asian travelers; he cites old Roman and Anglo-Saxon laws regarding moneylending and family relationships; he reveals the superiority of Christianity by comparing it with the ancient gods (Thor, Odun, and Woden) of the Scandinavians. Egyptian religious rites were cited for comparison with the Jewish religion. Greek and Roman hairdressing styles were described to elucidate 1 Pet. 3:3.

## Sermon Illustrations Used by Adam Clarke

| Source | 41 Edited Sermons | 19 Shorthand Sermons | Total All Sermons | Rank |
|---|---|---|---|---|
| Common Life Experiences | 54 | 28 | 82 | 1 |
| Bible | 64 | 12 | 76 | 2 |
| Science, Health | 48 | 2 | 50 | 3 |
| Nature | 39 | 3 | 42 | 4 |
| Personal | 12 | 27 | 39 | 5 |
| Ancient History and Ancient Customs | 30 | 5 | 35 | 6 |
| History and Church History | 22 | 2 | 24 | 7 |
| The Church World, World Religions | 11 | 7 | 18 | 8 |
| Current Events, Politics, Government, etc. | 9 | 2 | 11 | 9 |
| Mythology | 4 | | 4 | 10 |
| Literature | 3 | | 3 | 11-12 |
| Theology/Philosophy | 3 | | 3 | 11-12 |
| *Totals* | 299 | 88 | 387 | |
| *Average per sermon* | 7.29 | 4.63 | 6.45 | |

One of Clarke's most fruitful sources for illustrations was *the Bible.* He skillfully supported Old Testament texts with illustrations from the New Testament and vice versa. For example, in preaching on "Christ Crucified" (1 Cor. 1:22-24), he relevantly uses the Tower of Babel incident, Moses in the wilderness, and Abraham in covenant with God.

When it came to *personal illustrations,* Clarke largely avoided them. When he did use an illustration from his own experience, the focus was on the persons or events he had observed and not upon himself. Perhaps more personal illustrations from his interesting life would have made his sermons even more effective, but the pulpit style of the day was against extensive use of personal illustrations.

While the art of masterful illustration was not the *forte* of Clarke, being able to draw illustrations from a vast number of subjects ranging from ancient Persian lore to the latest medical discovery was a great strength in his preaching. Almost anyone could go to hear Clarke preach and expect to learn something new.

Clarke's style of preaching was uniquely his own. Today's minister will probably find inductive proofs more suited to late 20th-century audiences than the rigid syllogistic deduction of Clarke. It was in the deductive argument part of the sermon that tedium raised itself on one elbow to slow down Clarke's sermons and distract some hearers. Nevertheless, Clarke models for us the power of proven truth. Deduction fit the scheme of his sermonizing quite well. And while today's preacher may not follow Clarke in every detail, Clarke's thorough, sound use of logic is a ringing rebuke to many of today's pulpiteers whose titillating titles and twinkle-tipped alliterations don't even make sense, let alone prove anything.

# 6

# Ethos and Unction Count, Too

Somehow the audience senses the character of the preacher during a sermon. And the preacher's character impresses the hearers for better or worse. This is as important as logic and good style and effective delivery. The Greeks of classical times called it *ethos,* or ethical proof. It is the phenomenon of a preacher bringing his own inner essence, character, virtues, and reputation to bear on the persuasive moment.

Aristotle coaches us at this point in *The Rhetoric.*

> Of proofs provided by the speech there are three kinds: one kind depending on the character of the speaker . . . Ethical proof is wrought when the speech is so spoken as to make the speaker credible; for we trust good men more . . . about everything; while, about things which do not admit of precision . . . we trust them absolutely. It is not true . . . that the moral worth of the speaker contributes nothing to his persuasiveness; nay, it might be said that almost the most authoritative of proofs is that supplied by character.[1]

The Roman, Quintilian, says that the most important requirement for the orator is "he must be a good man."[2]

The ideal of classical times was "a good man speaking well."

The early Christian preachers, so often formed by the great Greek and Latin rhetorical traditions, were even more inclined to stress the preacher's life, character, and credibility as more important than eloquence.[3] Augustine in *De Doctrina Christiana* cited these ethical requirements for the Christian expositor: piety, reverence, fortitude, prudence, cleanness of heart. This says nothing of argumentation, of eloquence, nor of exegetical skill, as important as these are. Augustine is telling us that all preaching skills may be nullified if the ethical impact made by the preacher's character is closer to that of Jesse James than Jesus Christ. The sermon is given "that they may believe" (cf. John 11:42). How can they believe if the preacher is not credible?

Two men were talking about a certain preacher. One noted that his homiletic style was not all he had hoped it would be. His companion replied, "Yes, but every time I hear him, I want to be better." He was talking about this elusive quality called *ethos*.

*Ethos,* or ethical proof, was one of the most convincing elements in Adam Clarke's preaching. He was well known, not only for his learning and his powerful preaching, but for his holy living. J. W. Etheridge, who knew Clarke very well, wrote:

> One great charm, that rendered his ministry so attractive was found in the well-known qualities of his own . . . holy life. . . . The gospel which he preached harmonized with his personal character. He lived the gospel. His life . . . was itself a ceaseless homily of things . . . pleasing unto God.[4]

Another writer said that people received Clarke's preaching so eagerly because they knew "he was ready to maintain his integrity with a martyr's faithfulness, and that he maintained his piety by an humble faith."[5] James Everett, a confidential friend of Clarke's, hailed this *ethical* dimension, saying his "private virtues will ever be green in the memory of the blessed in the records of the miltant church."[6] His preaching "had all the more heart in it from the experience which he himself enjoyed of the saving power of the truth. Why did his hearers feel so? It was because the preacher had felt first. He came before them full-dressed in the mantle of salvation, with his lamp burning."[7]

What preacher could not profit from meditating on the example of Clarke's "persuasion by character."

## UNCTION IS . . .

Most preachers find it hard to define the"unction" or "anointing" of the Holy Spirit in preaching. Nevertheless they can tell you what it is like not to have it when preaching—it is painful, lonely, desperate, discouraging beyond description. W. E. Sangster describes unction as

> that mystic plus in preaching which no one can define and no one (with any spiritual sensitivity at all) can mistake. Men have it, or they do not have it. It is a thing apart from good sermon outlines, helpful spiritual insights, wise understanding, or eloquent speech. It can use all these media—and dispense with them. It is rare . . . and unspeakably precious.[8]

Sangster further observes, "Unction comes only on praying. Other things precious to a preacher come of prayer and something else. Unction comes only of praying. If nothing else revealed the poverty of our secret prayers, the absence of unction would."[9]

If prayer is the principle factor in Spirit-anointed preaching, it is no wonder that those who heard Adam Clarke remarked again and again about the unusual degree of unction which punctuated his preaching. Clarke was a man of prayer. As one close friend observed, "The Bible was his one book and prayer his continual exercise; he frequently read it on his knees, and often watered it with his tears."[10] His son Joseph wrote of his father:

> He never entered the pulpit but with the conviction, that if God did not help him by the influence of his Spirit, his heart must be hard and his mind dark . . . without unction and without fruit. For this influence he besought the Lord with strong crying and tears; and he was seldom, if ever left to himself.[11]

James Everett said of Clarke, "No herald of salvation ever sounded forth his message with greater faithfulness or fervour . . . and few ministers in modern times have been more honoured by the extraordinary unction of the Holy Spirit."[12]

What all this means is even better seen in the description given by a man when he first heard Adam Clarke preach. Clarke was preaching on the love of God; and when this great truth began to move his soul, he became almost irresistible. The new hearer remarked:

> It was then that I witnessed, and felt too, how this man could master and control the entire intellect and heart of a great congregation by the simple, honest, and earnest exhibition of the faith. . . . We were all subdued; the tears of repentance, the uplifted eyes of prayer, the swelling emotion of triumphal joy, which longed to give utterance in one loud thunder of thanksgiving, all showed how powerful is the uncorrupted gospel when preached aright.[13]

It was such demonstrations of the Holy Spirit's power that caused Clarke frequently to say after such services, "I would not have missed coming to this place for five hundred pounds. I got my own soul blessed, and God blessed the people."[14]

Sangster said, in the passage cited earlier, that divine unction is "unspeakably precious." It was so to Clarke. While on his frequent preaching journeys, he faithfully wrote to his wife, Mary. Again and again in those letters he related how God gave him liberty to preach or how the Spirit blessed the people. After preaching at Oldham Street Chapel in Manchester, he wrote:

> Perhaps I never preached as I did this morning. O, Mary, I had the kingdom of God opened to me, and the glory of the Lord filled the whole place. Toward the conclusion the cries were great. It was with great difficulty that I could get the people persuaded to leave. . . . Though the press was immense, yet scarcely one seemed willing to go away, and those who were in distress were unable to go. Some of the preachers . . . prayed with them, no one rested till they were healed. God has done a mighty work.[15]

**Adam Clarke's boyhood home**

The church which once housed the elementary school where Adam attended every other day. He and his brother Tracy had to take turns alternating daily farm work and schoolwork.

Burnside—the farm house where young Adam Clarke first heard a Methodist preacher preach full salvation.

City Road Chapel, London. Here Wesley and Clarke both preached often, and both are buried in its cemetery.

# 7

# Sermon Shaping

The importance of sermon structure blared at me from the television screen. A well-known TV preacher was sounding off. You could sense that he had been so busy making commercials and fine tuning a video extravaganza that he had not had time to fine tune his sermon. It is very possible that his sermon preparation had consisted of reaching for the trusty *Cruden's Concordance* and finding a string of scriptures that had certain words in them. His sermon was a running comment on scriptures violently wrenched from their contexts. It was a hodgepodge of contradiction and irrelevance. Since the sermon made no sense at all, the celebrity could not rely on cogency and logic to carry the day, so he covered up his logical laziness with emotional epithets like, "Bless God, I'd rather live in a shack with cracks so wide you could throw a cat through the wall and have Jesus than to have all the gold in Fort Knox and be without Him."

*Arrangement* is our term for what the ancients called *dispositio*. It refers to the technique of skillfully arranging the various elements of the speech or sermon in the most effective way. "The discourse is not to be a mere agglomeration of statements, but an organism, fitted to move as one thought."[1]

Many preachers neglect this art as "unspiritual," or else they cheapen it by making the sermon a flippant "flailing away at the obvious with three alliterative points."[2] But to make the Word of God of none effect through lack of attention to structure is not in the same league as dropping a pop-up in the church softball game.

Proper arrangement has many benefits, including the following:

1. It produces a sermon that makes sense. It serves logic.

2. It is more easily remembered by both hearer and speaker.

3. It makes the message clear.

4. It makes the message relevant. "The 'granite faces' in our congregations are due to irrelevant preaching."[3]

5. It serves to *focus* the sermon on the subject at hand.

6. It makes the call to "decision" more effective.

Adam Clarke's sermon arrangement keyed more on the logical sequence of ideas than upon artistic arrangement. Cute alliteration he never used, nor eye-boggling titles. Nevertheless, the flow of meaningful arrangement is observable in most of the sermons. We shall look at his use of the introduction, the body, and the conclusion of sermons. Then we shall study his outlining and investigate the time factor in his preaching.

## THE SERMON INTRODUCTION

Clarke's typical introduction, in the published sermons, was 989 words in length or slightly less than ⅛ of

87

the sermon length of 8,102 words. Typically Clarke's introductions did three tasks.

## 1. *Announced the Gravity and Importance of the Subject Matter of the Text*

The first words of the sermon "Love to God and Man, the Fulfilling of the Law and the Prophets" are:

> The love we owe to God and man, the subject of these verses, is of the very greatest importance, and should be well understood by every man, as we are assured by our Lord himself that the whole of religion is comprised in thus loving God and our neighbor.[4]

## 2. *Explained the Historical Setting, Biblical Context, and Basic Meaning of the Text*

To do this, Clarke used paraphrases, short illustrations, and word studies. This part of the introduction was never omitted, and he spent the bulk of his introductory ration of words on this matter.

## 3. *Told the Audience the Scope of the Sermon*

He told them clearly what he was going to make of the subject. This he did, usually, by spelling out carefully the outline he was about to preach. For example, in his sermon on Rom. 1:16-17, he closes the introduction with:

> In considering the general subject of the text I shall inquire:
>
> I. What is the Gospel of Christ?
> II. Why is the apostle not ashamed of it?—It brought him salvation.
> III. What was the agency by which the saving tendency of the gospel is applied?—The power of God.
> IV. For whom were these benefits designed?—Jews and Gentiles.
> V. How are they secured?—By faith.[5]

In "The Glory of the Latter Days," he closes the introduction by giving a purpose statement followed by:

> I shall . . .
> I. Consider what is meant by the words, "It shall come to pass afterward."
> II. The prediction, "I will pour out my spirit upon all flesh;" and
> III. The consequences, "They shall prophesy," etc.
> IV. What is the deliverance or salvation that shall be the result?[6]

Clarke's introductions are not scintillating to the modern, entertainment-oriented ear. But to the serious-minded hearer the direction of the sermon was clear as a road map. Clarke would agree with David H. C. Read in believing that meaningful preaching springs from "knowing the Scriptures and the power of God and not from new-found skills in titillating the topical."[7]

Nevertheless, most modern preachers might seek for a bit more "sparkle" in their introductions than Clarke generally displayed. Further, some rhetoricians question the sharing the outline with the audience early in the speech. Their concern is that it weakens the factor of suspense as the sermon unfolds.

## THE BODY OF THE SERMON

Clarke used a variety of structural models in the construction of the body of the sermon. Sometimes he developed a syllogistic argument based on the text, history, experience, literature, and the Church in the first part of the body and followed that with a phrase-by-phrase exposition of the Bible passage nailing down the truth with the final authority. At other times he followed a Pauline pattern of dealing with *doctrine* first and *practice* second. At other times he used a purely expository pattern with the scriptural clauses themselves serving as the main points.

Clarke's general sequence in arrangement of (1) God's holiness, justice, and goodness, (2) man's contrasting sinfulness,[8] (3) God's gracious offer of salvation in Christ, and (4) the evangelistic appeal is demonstrated in "The Plan of Human Redemption."[9]

The text is Gal. 4:4-7, a text that we know Clarke preached from at least three times.

> But when the fulness of the time had come, God sent forth His Son, made of a woman, made under the Law, to redeem those who were under the Law, so that we might receive the adoption of sons. And because you are sons, God has sent forth the Spirit of his Son into your hearts, crying, Abba, Father. Therefore you are no longer a slave, but a son; and if a son, then you are an heir of God through Christ. [Clarke's translation]

The thesis or proposition of the sermon is: God in His wisdom, holiness, justice, and goodness prescribed the Incarnation and Atonement through Christ and offers adoption with full privileges into the family of God. Since man is fallen, cut off from the family, and wretchedly sinful, he should deplore his sins and eagerly accept the offer of adoption.

In the introduction, God is described as too wise to err, too holy to do wrong, and too good to be unkind. Thus the wisdom, holiness, justice, and goodness of God are established. The subsequent development of the body of the sermon is:

I. God's Nature Applied to Human Redemption
    A. Man, made in union with God, part of the heavenly family.
    B. Man, fallen, lost union with God and familial rights.
    C. God purposes to restore man to sonship by adoption.
    D. Jesus Christ born of a woman.
    E. The mystery of the Incarnation.
    F. The benefits extend to all.

II. But Why Should Christ Suffer?
  A. He purposed to do so for man's benefit.
  B. It was right and necessary.
  C. It was required for atonement.
  D. It was God's will.

III. In What State Was Man to Render All This Necessary?
  A. He was out of the family and cut off from its rights.
  B. Illustration of family rights and adoption.
  C. He was under the law, under its curse and condemnation.

IV. Privileges of the Adopted Sons (Heirs) of God
  A. Negative privilege (removal of guilt, etc.)
  B. Positive privilege (witness of Spirit, etc.)

V. All of This Is "Through Christ" (v. 7)

Conclusion: a series of propositions which *summarize* the sermon, *confirm* the proofs, and offer an *appeal* to those who will "deplore" their sins and be adopted into the family of God.

One thing to note with care is how each of the main points more or less naturally unfold from the previous one.

In "The Doctrine of Holiness," a sermon preached in London, August 11, 1816, Clarke uses this development.

*Text:* Psalm 51:10-12

Create in me a clean heart, O God; and renew a right spirit within me. Cast me not away from thy presence, and take not thy holy spirit from me. Restore unto me the joy of thy salvation, and uphold me with thy free spirit.

*Thesis or Proposition:* Men and women are hopelessly lost in sin and can only be saved through the God who can "recreate" man in righteousness and true holiness.

*Introduction:*
A. "Solemn importance" of the text

B. General explanation of text

C. Nature of the "psalm" as literature

*Body:*
   I. "Create in me a clean heart"—original, and acts of, sin
   II. "Renew a right spirit within me"—God can purify the inner man.
   III. "Restore unto me the joy of thy salvation; and uphold me with thy free spirit"—perseverance in purity required.
   IV. "Cast me not away from thy presence; and take not thy Holy Spirit from me"—to have the presence of God we must have the Spirit of God.

*Conclusion:* "Uphold me with thy free Spirit."

As seen in earlier chapters, the main points were buttressed with: word studies; theological, historical, and experiential arguments; illustrations from experience, life, and the Bible; and quotations from the classics, the Church Fathers, literature, and the Bible.

# CLARKE'S CONCLUSIONS

Clarke used a variety of concluding styles. The occasion, content of the sermon, and the leadership of the Spirit prescribed the form of conclusion.

## 1. *The Pastoral Conclusion*

In a pastoral, as opposed to an evangelistic, message Clarke would reach the climactic peak of the sermon in the body of the sermon, usually in the last main heading. The conclusion then became a pleasing glide back to earth and ended with a word of encouragement, a verse of scripture, a benediction, a part of the creed or liturgy, or a poem.

## 2. *The Summary Conclusion*

Sometimes Clarke's conclusion was a summary of the content and the clinching of the argument of the sermon. This frequently came in a list of declarations which could hardly be denied. He used the summary conclusion for both evangelistic and pastoral sermons.

In the *introduction* Clarke presented his outline in brief. In the *body* he expounded, explained, and proved it. In the *conclusion* he summarized and restated it. This was not with the "tin ring" of the old saw, "Tell them what you are going to tell them, tell them, tell them what you told them"; but Clarke's pattern did have the thoroughness it implies.

## 3. *The Stewardship Appeal Conclusion*

During the last few years of Clarke's life many, if not most, of his sermons were "occasional sermons." The dedication of a new church (with its debt), the missionary anniversary, the Bible Society offering, Methodist medical and social relief funds, the Sunday Schools, and other such "good causes" required an extraordinary fund raiser, and Clarke's reputation in this area was unrivaled. He called himself the "packhorse" of every Methodist charity.

A charity service presented a problem. Clarke would not spend a whole sermon on raising money. Rather at these occasions he preached the gospel. He would preach on salvation by faith, the Atonement, the witness of the Spirit, the doctrine of sanctification. Then, he would take the last few minutes of the sermon usually spent on the conclusion to say something about the offering to be taken. He never spoke of the fund raising more than three or four minutes. He trusted the people to give—and they did. Usually he made the financial appeal fit right in to the logical flow of the sermon. For example, in reducing

Clarke's sermon in behalf of the Ladies Lying-In Hospital[10] (a Methodist institution for destitute expectant mothers in London) to an argument, we see the flow of logic goes like this:

> God calls us to "reason" about our sinfulness (Isa. 1:18).
>
> Such reasoning reveals that God reaches down to us in loving condescension in Christ, offering us full salvation of which we are totally unworthy.
>
> We should, therefore, seek this if we have it not; and if we have it, we should follow Christ our pattern and give in loving condescension to the poor women of the lying-in charity.

Preaching on the Missionary Anniversary in London in 1820, his sermon's development was:

> God is love, and He has shown His love to us through Christ's atonement.
>
> We have benefited being redeemed by love, therefore we are indebted to share this love to all men everywhere.
>
> You can do this by giving to the missionary offering today.

In each of these cases Clarke (as was his custom) made an evangelistic sermon on redemption out of the "occasional" occasion.

### 4. *The Evangelistic Conclusion*

What appears to have been Clarke's most effective closing was the evangelistic conclusion. The technique used so effectively was a rush of unavoidable, undeniable, inescapable rhetorical questions. First, Clarke would energetically *prove* the holiness of God, the wretched sinfulness of man, and the gracious offer of full salvation through Christ. Then, with these proven propositions he would query, Who has excuse for not seeking God now?

The sermon "Experimental Religion and Its Fruits" offers a good example. The text is Phil. 1:9-11. The logic unfolds in this manner:

94

Inward sin, the carnal nature, corrupts men—even the justified.

In entire sanctification inward sin, the carnal nature, is destroyed through the purifying power of the Holy Spirit.

It is God's love that makes sanctification available, and it is
His will to sanctify you now; therefore, you should seek
holiness *now*.

These points are emphasized, explained, and proven
for 5,300 words; then Clarke presses the urgency of holiness, nearly overwhelming his hearers by bringing a rule to
bear on their minds, hearts, and conscience which admits
of no evasion and no appeal. In a series of 16 unanswerable
questions Clarke appeals, challenges, and convinces the
hearers.

> And now . . . art thou willing to have this apostolic
> prayer fulfilled to thee? Art thou weary of that carnal
> mind which is enmity to God? Canst thou be happy
> whilst thou art unholy? Dost thou know anything of
> God's love to thee? Dost thou not know that he has
> given his Son to die for thee? Dost thou love him in
> return for his love? Hast thou even a little love to him?
> And canst thou love him a little, without desiring to
> love him more? Dost thou not feel that thy happiness
> grows in proportion to thy love and subjection to him?
> Dost thou not wish to be happy? And dost thou not
> know that holiness and happiness are as inseparable as
> sin and misery? Canst thou have too much happiness
> or too much holiness? Canst thou be made holy and
> happy too soon? Art thou not weary of a sinful heart?
> Are not thy bad tempers, anger, peevishness, fretful-
> ness, covetousness, and the various unholy passions
> that too often agitate thy soul, a source of misery and
> woe to thee? And canst thou be unwilling to have them
> destroyed? Arise, then, and shake thyself from the
> dust, and call upon thy God! . . . he cannot be more
> willing to save thee in any future time, than he is now
> . . . the carnal mind . . . he is willing this moment to
> destroy.[11]

In one recorded climax of a sermon Clarke pictured

Christ in the process of creating a vast new galaxy of planets. But in the middle of all this He (Christ) heard a wretched sinner cry, "Jesus, Son of David, have mercy on me" (cf. Mark 10:47; Luke 18:38). Christ, in Clarke's story, immediately dropped the task of creating new worlds in order to rush to the lowly sinner's aid. The congregation was overwhelmed with a new realization of God's love.[12]

James Dixon, a distinguished Methodist leader, said that when Clarke had finished his argument, he came down with tremendous force in the conclusion. "He concentrated the truth he had been uttering into one focus. His declamation in the latter part of the sermon was overwhelming. I have seen a congregation transported by his power and force. Some were weeping, some smiling, some shouting for joy."[13]

Whichever style of conclusion Clarke used, it was for him the "action step." His conclusion almost invariably called for decision and action—and he hadn't even heard of psychomotor objectives.

Clarke's conclusions were generally brief—564 words on the average. If Clarke spoke at 135 words per minute, he used about four minutes to preach the conclusion.

## STRUCTURAL PROPORTION AND TIME IN CLARKE'S SERMONS

Computed at the rate of 135 words per minute (wpm), Clarke's sermons average almost exactly 60 minutes. Clarke's proportioning of time for the various structural components of the sermon varied according to the subject, the text, and the audience. But averaging his proportioning of his sermons, we get this overview of his pattern.

## Table 1

### Length and Proportion of Adam Clarke's Sermons

| | Word Length | | | | Time Length at 135 wpm | | | |
|---|---|---|---|---|---|---|---|---|
| | Intro-duction | Body | Con-clusion | Full Sermon | Intro-duction | Body | Con-clusion | Full Sermon |
| A. 41 Edited Sermons | 1,083 | 7,475 | 651 | 9,209 | 8 | 55 | 5 | 68 |
| B. 19 Shorthand Sermons | 787 | 4,550 | 376 | 5,713 | 6 | 33 | 3 | 42 |
| C. Difference Between A & B* | 296 | 2,925 | 275 | 3,496 | 2 | 22 | 2 | 26 |
| All 60 Sermons | 989 | 6,549 | 564 | 8,102 | 7 | 49 | 4 | 60 |

*The shorthand sermons were significantly shorter than the edited sermons. Two factors bear on this concern. James Everett, editor of the first edition of the sermons, says that (1) Clarke expanded the edited sermons, and (2) the person who took the other sermons down in shorthand missed part of the addresses. Thus, the average struck by comparing the edited and shorthand sermons may be reasonably accurate.

*Introduction*
> Statement of importance and rele-     *989 words*
>      vance of the subject/text     *7 minutes*
> Explanation of text
> Citing the scope and outline of the sermon

*Body*
> Expository/logical development of     *6,549 words*
>      the subject-text     *49 minutes*

*Conclusion*
> Summary/appeal     *564 words*
>          *4 minutes*

Table 1 shows further detail on Clarke's sermon shaping.

Few preachers can hold the attention of a congregation for an hour the way Clarke did. But his successful and sensible mode of sermon shaping could rescue many "wilderness wanderers" who are afoot at 11:15 on Sunday mornings. No small part of Clarke's general success is accounted for by clear, rational sermon construction.

# 8

# Words About the Word:
# Adam Clarke's Sermon Style

What preacher has not, with the upturned faces of his flock in his mind's eye and tears in his physical eyes, prayed, *O God, give me the right words. Help me say it in a way that will touch them.* It is soul passion looking for handles that makes sermon style an urgent challenge.

Some seem to think that the only truly spiritual use of the gift of language is to simply blurt out whatever you feel. While there is value in spontaneity, the biblical preacher should regard style as the instrument "through which ideas are made meaningful; it clothes the reason and emotion of the speaker in words that will have influence."[1]

With Wallace Fisher we must face the question, "Can God be patient . . . with preachers who, because of sloth, will not dig out the right words and labor into the night and get up early in the morning to put the right words together to communicate his Word persuasively?"[2] The effective preacher must toil at the task of mastering his own language. He or she must work with words until the resulting sermon "turns men's ears into eyes."[3] Unless a preacher is willing to work on style, his or her sermons are apt to be a jumble of sentence fragments, broken thoughts, and syntactical quagmires from which there is no graceful escape.

## THE QUALITIES OF STYLE

Xenophon tells of a great party in celebration of the Panathenaic Games. A man appears at the door of the banquet hall and announces: "You all know that I am a jester; and so I have come here . . . thinking it more of a joke to come to your dinner uninvited than to come by invitation."[4] Style, like the jester, usually comes uninvited. It is the preacher's own unique way of putting his thoughts and feelings into language. Everyone's style is different and should faithfully reflect the man and his message.

Although every preacher has his own style, certain qualities are required for effective style. The qualities frequently listed in books on preaching or speech include: clarity, simplicity, appropriateness, correctness, and beauty.

## ADAM CLARKE'S GENERAL STYLE

### 1. *Clarity and Simplicity*

As Philo Buck counsels, "The highest ends can be reached by the simplest means; and this is one very great secret in style."[5] Adam Clarke preached according to this principle. Like John Wesley he preached "plain truth to plain people." He advised his fellow preachers, "We had better be as simple as we can in the terms that express the salvation of the soul."[6]

Simplicity and clarity are married in the best sermons, and there is a difference between forceful simplicity and clarity, and boring blandness. The stylish sermon is clear, and sometimes the most ornamental metaphor is the path to making the abstract simple and clear. Clarke seems to have been coached by Aristotle's advice: "Let excellence of style . . . consist in its being clear."[7]

Clarke's sermons, though given extemporaneously without notes, were carefully thought out and logically arranged. This in itself contributed to the clear and simple style of Adam Clarke. Clarke exemplified Quintilian's maxim which urged the speaker not only to be so clear and simple that he could be understood, but to so speak "that he [the listener] may not be able not to understand us."[8]

Many of Clarke's hearers marveled that so learned a man could preach such clear and simple sermons. But Clarke was not preaching to dazzle and delight; he preached to narrow the gap between God and his hearers. He preached to move men Godward—not to make himself admired.

In an effort to further test Clarke's simplicity and clarity, I selected 15 random samples from the sermons and submitted them to the Dale, Chall, Clare readability test. Here we discover that Clarke, one of the most learned men of his times, preached on the junior high level much of the time. The sermons which Clarke edited after the fact for publication were nearly two grade levels higher in language difficulty than the sermons taken down in shorthand. The edited sermons, honed for a wider, and in many cases a more sophisticated, audience, were still simple; but added word studies, quotations, and the like raised the readability to the 10th grade level. The sermons taken down as they were preached fell on the 8th grade level. See Table 1 for a summary of the readability study. Refer to Appendix 5 for a fuller charting of the readability of Clarke's sermons.

## Table 1

### Readability of Clarke's Sermons

| | Number of Words | Number of Sentences | Number of Words Not on the Dale List | Average Number of Words per Sentence | Dale Score | Raw Score | Grade Level |
|---|---|---|---|---|---|---|---|
| Five Samples, Shorthand Sermons | 581 | 26 | 81 | 22.3 | 13.9 | 6.94 | 8* |
| Ten Samples, Edited Sermons | 1,135 | 41 | 199 | 27.7 | 17.5 | 7.87 | 10 |
| Grand Total, All Sermons | 1,716 | 67 | 280 | 25.6 | 16.3 | 7.40 | 9 |

*This means that a person with 8th grade reading skills could "read" Clarke's sermons with 80% comprehension.

The one factor in the readability formula that made Clarke's intelligibility level as high as it is was his tendency to use long sentences. It is, of course, less than conclusive to test 160-year-old sermons by today's intelligibility standards. But it does give us some measure of the clarity and simplicity with which Clarke preached. Perhaps the best evidence of clarity and simplicity is given by those who heard him. One man writing about a sermon preached in Belfast recalled, "He . . . spoke his experience with great simplicity testifying of his happy enjoyment of salvation by faith . . . of which he felt assured, as well by rational demonstration, as by the witness of the Spirit."[9]

One of his fellow preachers observed of Clarke:

> He possessed an astonishing power of gathering together rays of light from the whole circuit of his knowledge, and pouring them in one bright beam upon any point. . . . His faculty in this respect was truly surprising, and gave an originality to his conceptions, and a strength to his arguing, and a body of such unexpected,

yet clear evidence of his facts, that delighted conviction was almost universally the result of his reasoning.[10]

Clarke, preaching in Lerwick in the Shetland Islands, drew this bemused comment from an old woman who came to the Methodist meetinghouse to hear him preach. "I had heard that Dr. Clarke was . . . very learned; but when I heard him, I found him just like any other man. I could understand every word he said."[11]

## 2. *Appropriateness and Correctness*

Clarke was a master of many languages; therefore, it is not surprising that he models for us correct usage. Though he is not infrequently wordy by today's standards, his usage, grammar, and syntax are nearly perfect—even in the shorthand sermons. Here he serves as a model for many of us who have to write a sentence three times to get it right.

Correct usage may not be the most important aspect of the sermon. If the content is erroneous, the logic self-contradictory, and the preacher's personality repelling, careful avoidance of infinitive splitting will not redeem the preacher's predicament. Nevertheless, correct usage can make the gospel clear and avoid bringing criticisms of sloth and ignorance into competition with the offer of divine grace.

In the matter of appropriateness Clarke again coaches us well. Appropriateness simply means that the style of the sermon (the language used) to be most effective must be appropriate to the subject, the occasion, the setting, and to the preacher who does the speaking. Clarke's sermons obeyed the laws of propriety. He never sought the sensational or the vulgar for the sake of attention-getting "as the manner of some is" today. He never imitated the style of the orators of the moment although then, as now, the practice was common. Clarke declared, "There is a great deal of fictitious character among the ministers of the present day. Formerly it was not so. Now they are aping Mr. ——— and Mr. ——— . . . the young men especially are quite a different race from their fathers. They are stiffened up and cut out by reading, study and mimicry til there is very little genuine natural character left. I abhor all aping,—I care not who the man is."[12]

### 3. *Beauty*

When Clarke began to preach sermons on his one message of full salvation now by grace through faith, the British pulpits were populated by preachers of pretty sermons. For the preceding 200 years British preachers yearned for eloquence. They so ornamented the sermon with tropes and figures and rhetorical devices that they preached the sermon for its own sake. Every sentence was loaded with metaphor, catachresis, litotes, asyndeton, tapinosis, and the like. Like Aristotle's sophist, Alcidamas, they did not use tropes and figures "as sauce for the meat, but as the meat itself."[13] The gospel was lost in the florid, luxuriant language in which it was figured, alluded to, and symbolized.

For such pulpit style Clarke had little patience. He declared,

> The simple and forcible method of preaching the gospel soon degenerates, and rhetoric or oratory is studied much more than divinity. A copious flow and elegance of language—words of splendid sound, imposing epithets, and striking figures and similes, are everywhere sought, in order to form harmonious sentences, and finely turned periods; a fustian language, misnamed *oratory,* is thus introduced into the church of Christ; but when the words of this are analysed, they are found, however musically arranged, to be destitute of force; so that a dozen of such expressions will labour

in vain to produce one single impressive idea that can illuminate the understanding, correct the judgment, or persuade the conscience either to hate sin or love righteousness. "How forcible are right words!" can never be applied to such sermons; they may please the giddy and superficial, but they neither edify the saint, nor bring conviction into the bosom of the sinner. And what redounds to their reproach and discredit is, they are flowers meanly stolen from the garden of others.[14]

Clarke did not labor incessantly at decorating his sermons. He preached plain truth in a moderate style. There was no engaging in the flowery language which "may be merely superficial, a glittering tinsel, which however much it may please the shallow-minded, cannot fail to disgust the judicious."[15] He deliberately refused to subject his preaching to the artificial sermon science of his day. "To reduce preaching to . . . science and . . . art is something of which my soul cannot form too horrid an idea."[16]

While Clarke did not court eloquence in order to impress, neither did he consort with crudity of expression, as some preachers seem impelled to do in order to show that they are just plain folks. Clarke used the moderate style in good taste.

The moderate or "middle" style of address is informal, yet has dignity and a moderate amount of beauty and grace. The "grand" style ranges from formal speech to the luxuriantly florid. The "plain" style is the vernacular. It is casual, street language with no attempt to make it beautiful or decorative. Clarke used the whole range at times but did most of his preaching in the moderate range.

Thus his sermons have a certain dignity and a rugged beauty about them. They contain rhetorical devices and ornament to a degree that harmonizes with simple good taste. The devices that intensify, convince, clarify, repeat and restate, add interest, emphasize, make concrete the abstract, add suspense, and build to climax are numerous in Clarke's sermons; but they are so naturally and skill-fully done that they are hardly noticeable. It was this kind of style that John Broadus described when he said, "Style is excellent when, like the atmosphere, it shows the thought, but itself is not seen."[17]

The study of Clarke's masterful use of language is so fascinating that it is hard to find a stopping place. We shall not explore all of Clarke's stylistic instruments with which he orchestrated great sermons. We shall limit this study to a sampling of them. About half of them have ominous-looking Latin names which are often pronounced improperly—it's hard to remember where the accent goes. Ominous as they look, they are not complex. Many preachers use them naturally without knowing or caring about their Latin labels.

## CLARKE'S SPECIFIC STYLE DEVICES

### 1. *The Periodic Sentence*

Like most great preachers Adam Clarke was a master of the periodic sentence. Andrew Blackwood observes that "the mastery of the periodic sentence affords a . . . con-clusive proof of a man's education and culture."[18] A pe-riodic sentence is one in which "ideas hang in the air like girders until all interconnections are locked by the final word."[19] That is, the sentence, in grammatical con-struction and meaning, is not complete until the final phrase is given. Using such sentences builds suspense and maintains interest. Even if the listener disagrees with you, he can't turn you off until he has heard the whole sentence. Here are examples from Clarke:

> Alas, that we must add, from this state of perfec-tion, excellence, and happiness, man fell![20]

> How strange, how disgraceful is it, that the words of the devil, and the wicked words of a lying world, and

antinomian maxims of fallen churches, or fallen Christians, should be implicitly believed, while the words of the living God are not credited.[21]

It is difficult not to stop here and point out the alliteration and consonance (note the clusters of *w, m,* and *l* sounds) which give the above periodic sentence pleasing rhythm and progression.

## 2. *Anaphora*

Perhaps Clarke's most powerful rhetorical device was combining the periodic sentence with anaphoric phrasing. *Anaphora* means "a bringing again." This is a repetition-for-emphasis device and a tool for intensifying the force of the sermon. Using it, the speaker begins a series of successive sentences or clauses with the same word or sound. Here's how it worked when Clarke combined periodic sentences with the anaphora device (italics added):

> *All* the exhortations, *all* the entreaties, *all* the counsels, *all* the promises, and *all* the threatenings contained in this sacred book, are founded on this principle.[22]

> Then *those* that are our enemies—*those* who are our bitterest enemies and persecutors—*those* who would be our tormentors, if they had us in their power —*those* who would direct against us their utmost malice, we should love even them.[23]

Clarke does not always combine the periodic sentence with anaphora. Here is an example of anaphora alone. Clarke is expounding on Ps. 15:3, "He . . . backbiteth not with his tongue."

> *He* foots not upon or with his tongue [a colloquialism well known to Clarke's hearers]. *He* is one who treats his neighbor with respect. *He* says nothing that might injure him. . . . *He* forges no calumny. *He* is author of no slander. *He* insinuates nothing.[24]

Sometimes Clarke used a sort of double or alternating

anaphoric construction. Here is an example from his sermon "True Happiness."

> *He feels* his weakness, and *looks* to God as his strength; *he feels* his bondage, and *looks* to God as his deliverer.[25]

## 3. *Epistrophe*

This is another intensifying, emphasizing device. It is ending successive clauses or sentences with the same word or words. Here is an example of simple epistrophe from Clarke's sermon "Promises to the Man Who Has Set His Love upon God."

> Every member must have piety for *himself;* he must have faith for *himself;* pardon and holiness for *himself.*[26]

In the following quotation Clarke combines epistrophe with anaphora, beginning clauses with the same word and ending clauses with the same word.

> But a Spirit, such as God, is unlimited; hence *his* power is *without bounds, his* mercy is *without bounds, his* goodness and his truth are *without bounds.*[27]

In the following sample Clarke combines all three devices considered so far—periodic sentences, anaphora, and epistrophe.

> *His* word says *No;* and *His* Spirit says, *No; His* church says, *No;* and *His* own eternal and loving nature says, *No.* God the Father will, *for* Christ's *sake, for* his own Name's *sake,* and *for* his Truth's *sake,* give his Holy Spirit to them that ask him.[28]

## 4. *Anadiplosis*

To use anadiplosis, you repeat early in a clause a significant word from the end of the preceding clause. Clarke used anadiplosis more sparingly than some other rhetorical instruments; but when he did use it, it brought a pleasing rhythm and an intensifying of the power of the sermon.

> You obey no longer than you *love;* you *love* no longer than you believe; you *believe* no longer than you are looking to Jesus.[29]

## 5. *Epanalepsis*

This is an echo device used as a pleasing play on words for emphasis. The speaker begins and ends a series of clauses with the same word. Clarke illustrates this device in speaking of the work of the Christian minister:

> The servant of Jesus Christ, *labours* before he begins to *labour; labours* most while he is *labouring;* and *labours* after he [is] done *labouring.*[30]

## 6. *Chiasmus*

*Chiasmus* means "a crossing" and is the name given the device whereby the speaker crosses the terms of one clause by reversing their order in the next. When properly used, this tool can so emphasize a contrast as to make it memorable. For example, consider J. F. Kennedy's famous chiasmus (taken from the 19th-century idea of Oliver Wendell Holmes):

> Ask not what your country can do for you: ask what you can do for your country.[31]

Clarke used quite a number of chiasmuslike sayings and several times used the pure chiasmus as in these two examples:

> The portion of the righteous is not for the wicked: the lot of the wicked is not that of the just.[32]

> Such is the God of Israel; and such is the Israel of the Lord.[33]

## 7. *Metaphor*

*Metaphor* means "a carrying across" and is the label given to describing something as if it were something else. For example: "All flesh is grass" (Isa. 40:6; cf. 1 Pet. 1:24).

Whereas it is the function of the chiasmus to clarify by *contrast,* it is the function of metaphor to clarify by *comparison.*

Adam Clarke used many metaphors, but he did not use them to excess. Satan is seen as a ravenous beast and Clarke challenges his hearers to "arise, grapple with the destroyer, and *pluck the prey out of his teeth.*"[34] The Koran is "a stagnant lake of asphaltic water," while the Bible is "living water . . . from Siloah's brook."

As in the example just cited, Clarke sometimes used double, triple, or quadruple metaphors to create an "image cluster." For example, in his sermon "Christ Crucified" he uses these metaphors: *"ocean* of learning," *"sink* of pollution," "a *whirlpool* to *engulf* Christianity," and "a *sink* of heathenism." In the same sermon the Jewish people who rejected Christ were *"caught in the trap* which they had laid," and they had fallen *"into a pit."* In another sermon legal restraint is seen as a *"bit"* and public authority has *"reins"*—thus a consistent image of horsemanship is sustained.

For Clarke, being delivered from temptation is "to be delivered from the *paw of the lion";* and this is "no small mercy," he says, combining metaphor and litotes. Further, hell becomes the *"ditch* of remediless perdition"; sin is a *"prison,"* happiness a *"cup,"* steps in logic *"links in a chain."* Misery is a *"harrow"* of the soul, God's love a *"fountain,"* and man is a *"transcript"* of God's own eternity. One metaphor that Clarke used would likely not be profitable for today's prophet—the love of God is called a *"girdle."*

## 8. *Simile*

Simile is a cousin to metaphor, clarifying by comparison. Like metaphor, it frequently functions to make the abstract concrete, and compares the known to the unknown. Here are some of Clarke's similes:

When some people pray, they rush "into the presence of God, *as the horse does into battle.*"[35] A Greek word for prayer means to "crouch down *as a dog before his master.*" Some Christian converts Clarke knew "drank in knowledge *as the thirsty land does the showers,*" and they became *"steady as steel.*"[36] In the parish workhouse "instances of real conversion are *as rare . . . as the black swan among birds.*"[37]

## 9. *Personification*

Many a limp sentence or paragraph can be rescued by giving some inanimate object or theory the qualities or action of a person. Adam Clarke knew this and livened some of his addresses with the following.

The doctrine of predestination was given personal qualities to its chagrin: "Can the Molochian doctrine of unconditional reprobation *look these Scriptures, or the incarnated Jesus in the face, and not hasten to hide itself in the pit of perdition.*"[38]

"Blasphemy *stalks abroad unmasked";* hope is to "be the *pioneer* of the soul"; the honest worker for God is to *"grasp* time by the *forelock";* death has a *"carrion breath";* the *"fiend* of war" has been chained; and *poverty* has *"tongue-tied"* some destitute Christians.

## 10. *Synecdoche and Metonymy*

Clarke used these popular tropes sparingly. They are types of metaphors in which you put the part for the whole or the whole for the part, the species for the genus and vice versa, the material for the object it constitutes (synecdoche), or substitute an associated item for the thing itself.[39]

"How many of our ancestors have been driven through Smithfield fires to heaven"[40] (a reference to martyrdom). The devil "counted on the destruction of Christianity by fire and sword,"[41] that is, through persecution and death or war. "The sword is put into its scabbard,"[42] meaning peace has come.

## 11. *Alliteration, Assonance, and Consonance*

Alliteration, as every preacher knows too well, is the repetition of the first letter or sound of two or more nearby words. Consonance is the repetition of internal consonant sounds. Assonance is the repetition or rhyming of internal vowel sounds. Clarke never used alliteration to outline a sermon. He used alliteration in combination with consonance which gave a certain pleasing rhythm to his prose. For example, a key paragraph of eight lines might contain 10 or more initial or internal $p$ or $s$ sounds. Sometimes he would use an alliterated pair in a short phrase. One of his favorites was "private ways and public haunts." Only one time in the 60 sermons did he stack up three alliterated words together. In that case he was citing the fickleness of female fashions and flailed at them in a fervid phrase about "fantastic, frippery fashions."[43] Clarke seldom used assonance, and used consonance and alliteration only as spice and seasoning to add interest; they were never the main dish itself.

## 12. *Anacoenosis*

I have never read of nor heard a preacher who used anacoenosis as effectively as Adam Clarke. This tool is the epitome of the intensifying devices. It occurs when the preacher heightens his style in urgent consultation with the hearers, and with frequent rhetorical questions gains an urgent mixture of intimacy and elegance.[44]

Clarke's use of this was explored in an earlier chapter when his sermon conclusions were considered. We noted that after laying out an airtight, logical, scriptural case for accepting God's offer of salvation, he would then bring a series of unavoidable rhetorical questions to bear on the decision that few honest hearers could resist. This was one of Clarke's most effective stylistic instruments with which he convinced men and women of their needs and brought them to a decision. He did not reserve this device for the conclusion only. He was likely to use it in clinching each main point in the sermon.

We will take time to cite only one of the many examples: In his sermon on Ps. 15:1-5 Clarke proposes to answer the question, "Who shall abide in thy tabernacle? who shall dwell in thy holy hill?" After establishing the requirements for heaven as suggested in verses 2-5, Clarke confronts the hearers with a call to decision via anacoenosis, the rush of urgent rhetorical questions.

> Let your conscience answer the following questions. Will a man . . . that does not speak the truth in his heart be saved? Will the backbiter and slanderer . . . get to heaven? Will he get there, in whose eyes the vile person is honourable; and he who fears the Lord despicable? Will he who breaks his word . . . get to heaven? . . . And do you expect to go to heaven with all your imperfections on your head? Then you are most awfully deceived. . . . Did Christ come to destroy the moral law? Does the gospel require holiness of heart and life? You know it does. And do you believe this word "Without holiness no man shall see God"? And what does this psalm require, but holiness of heart and life which the gospel everywhere requires? Is the . . . gospel . . . against a holy life? Then you must receive the grace of the gospel, that the . . . Spirit of life may make you free from the law of sin and death.[45]

Perhaps we should note again that to Clarke and to all preachers, style is not the most important factor in preaching. *What* you proclaim is more important than how you proclaim it. Neither how nor what, however, is unimportant.

If the complexity of the factors of style in Clarke's preaching discourages you, remember that Adam Clarke was a gifted genius at language usage. Further, even Clarke's style could have been more appropriately garnished. Richard Watson and Jabez Bunting, two of Clarke's contemporaries, preached more artistically than Adam. I have cited many figures and tropes, but this is not to say that they were strewn knee-deep throughout the sermons. They were somewhat sparse, with some dry stretches in between.

Two mistakes could be made in responding to this chapter: (1) trying to make every line in a sermon twinkle with rhetoric; (2) writing out sermons in full, trying on phrases, and memorizing sermons until naturalness is blown away like an October maple leaf.

With these cautions noted, it is still true that the study of effective language usage is a lifelong challenge to the evangelical preacher. Wallace Fisher points out the goal. He says preachers should "use words honestly, as a friend speaks them; skillfully, as the novelist employs them; insightfully, as the poet chooses them; carefully, as the advocate speaks them; clear-headedly as the teacher uses them; and graciously as the lover whispers them."[46]

# 9

## Holiness?
## Adam Clarke Preached Little Else

Adam Clarke was a man of one message—full salvation now by grace through faith. The part of this message that received his greatest emphasis was the second work of grace—sanctification.

Holiness was the major or minor theme of 38 of the 60 sermons. And it was at least given honorable mention in all of them. Even in sermons in which one might not at first expect holiness to be stressed, it emerges as one of the main themes. For example, his sermon on "The Doctrine of Repentance" is not limited to the new birth. Clarke declared that one reason repentance is so important is that it is a doorway to sanctification, which is God's will for all believers. This became one of the main points of the sermon. Even when he was a guest speaker at the fund raiser, Clarke usually presented the whole plan of salvation, stressing sanctification.

Presenting sanctification as part of the whole counsel of God was the great strength of Clarke's preaching on holiness. Never in the 60 sermons did he take a single aspect of holiness and present it out of context. That is, he never treated sanctification without also discussing justification, and usually glorification. Salvation was three-tiered for Clarke: justification, sanctification, glorification. In the sermons in which holiness was the major theme, Clarke nearly always presented holiness in an even wider context. He started with a just, holy, and good God, moved to the sinfulness of man, and from there to justification, sanctification, and glorification. Sanctification received the lion's share of attention, although justification was cited as the greatest miracle. When in a sermon Clarke wasn't preaching on holiness, he was leading up to it.

The stress on sanctification was particularly strategic. The people Clarke preached to were living on the ebb tide of the Reformation which had stressed justification by faith so strongly that by now it had solidified into a theological provincialism. Still echoing across the channel were Luther's teachings. Some of them that got isolated and became more like stumbling blocks than stepping-stones were:

1. Man is a horse. If he is ridden by God, he is ridden to heaven. If he is ridden by the devil, he rides into hell.

2. If on Sunday morning you see two men, one in a ditch dead drunk from Saturday night revelry, and the other on his way to church with a Bible under his arm, there is no way to know which one is the Christian.

3. As far as sin goes, even the best Christian will have a Romans 7 struggle on his hands as long as he or she lives.

Meanwhile from the mountains of Switzerland, Calvin was bugling all sorts of good news like "Sin is the instrument God uses to damn those He predestines to hell." When Beza seized this and set it in concrete, and later when it was decorated with the "tulip of Dort," a strange picture of the Christian life appeared.

By now even the Westminster Confession, the creed of creeds, declared that even the regenerate would sin in word, thought, and deed as long as they lived. All this reduced the life of those with a religious turn of mind to seek some sort of justification by faith (if they were so predestined) and to search for some evidence of it in their lives. Their best religious leaders left them at the gate of justification.

There was nothing more to do but thank God for what He had done for them. Evangelism was rather beside the point with the ghost of predestination looming so ominously on the horizon. And since good works could not save them, Adam Clarke observed, they were content to have no good works at all. Further, how happy can you be, thinking that no matter how you yearn for holiness that you must always be a slave to sin?

Into this malaise strolled John Wesley, Adam Clarke, and Company, Bibles in hand, declaring fearlessly to one and all, "The tulip of Dort is a vile (or at least imperfect) flower. The Bible speaks of holiness of heart here and now." The Methodists expounded the Word, teaching that lifelong slavery to sin was not the Christian's prospect. Carrying about a corrupt heart was not required—rather, it was forbidden. The springs of the soul can flow crystal clear and clean. The revival was on—people hungering for holiness, guided by pure doctrine, sought and found it.

One of Adam Clarke's favorite ways of treating holiness was to tell believers that justification is what God has done *for* us, but you must now hear the Word about

117

what God wants to do *in* us. He did not belittle justification, but he stressed sanctification more—because it was the need of the hour. He said, "Many talk much, and well, of what Christ has done FOR us: but how little of what he is to do IN us! . . . He was incarnated, suffered, died and rose again . . . FOR us that he might reconcile us to God; . . . [and] blot out our sin."[1] What God wants to do *in* us, Clarke asserted, is "wash the polluted heart, destroy every foul and abominable desire, all tormenting and unholy tempers . . . make the heart his throne, fill the soul with light, power, and life."[2]

The problem, Clarke pointed out, was that even the best writers of the previous 100 years generally "leave the people in the article of justification by faith. . . . People saw nothing further to be obtained, nothing further to be sought."[3] The result was "the rest of their lives seemed to be spent in thanksgiving to God, that they had received the unspeakable gift; their religious feelings and zeal became inactive; the earnestness to bring others to the grace they had received began to cease."[4] Clarke thought the genius of the Methodist movement was that there was no stopping place. After conversion a person was called to sanctification, and after that continual growth in order to stay among the redeemed.

## What Adam Clarke Preached on the Subject of Holiness

Clarke called the second work of grace by various names: sanctification, purity, Christian perfection, holiness, complete holiness, complete sanctification, and the fullness of the gospel of Jesus. Following is a synthesis of the points in the doctrine which Clarke stressed in his sermons.

118

### 1. *God's Word Is the Authority upon Which the Doctrine Is Based*

The truth of the doctrine does not depend, according to Clarke, on experience of men and women. It stands on God's Word. "Suppose not one [person] could be found in all the churches of Christ whose heart was purified . . . who loved God and man with all his regenerated powers, yet the doctrine of Christian perfection would still be true"[5] because of God's Word.

Some of the scriptures from which Clarke preached holiness include: Ps. 51:10-12; Ezek. 36:25-27; Matt. 5:9-10, 47; John 4:8-11; 7:38-39; 17; Acts 15:8-9; 1 Cor. 6:20; 2 Cor. 6:16-18; 7:1; Gal. 5:6; Eph. 2:4-5; 3:14-21; 4:24; Col. 1:27-28; 2:10; Titus 2:14; Heb. 9:13-14; 1 Pet. 1:18-19; 2:24; 3:18; 5:10-11; 1 John 1:7; Rev. 7:14.

### 2. *The Doctrine Is Verified by Human Experience*

The truth of the doctrine of entire sanctification in this life is affirmed by the Scriptures, and that is enough, but it is also verified by human experience. "If I had no other proof of the truth of this doctrine than . . . the testimony of those who profess faith in Christ Jesus," Clarke said to the congregation in City Road Chapel, London, on April 30, 1820, "I should conceive that this was sufficient to satisfy every reasonable mind."[6] To a Christian who asked him if there were any examples of sanctified people he could meet, Clarke told the good man to seek the experience and he would soon know one such person firsthand.

### 3. *The Holiness of God Is the Ground of the Call for Man to Be Holy*

Clarke repeatedly cited a holy, just, and good God as man's Creator who in love calls man to fulfill his destiny by being like his Maker. "God is holy," he declared, "and this is the eternal reason why all his people should be holy."[7] "From a simple, pure affection of love, he made man for the manifestation of his own perfections . . . that he might be made a partaker of his holiness and . . . his happiness."[8]

## 4. *The Need for Holiness Springs from Man's Fallen State*

That man was created in holiness Clarke believed and preached. But man fell, and "the grandeur of the ruins shows the unrivalled excellence and perfection of the original building."[9] Though man was "fearfully and wonderfully made," declares Clarke, he became "fearfully and wonderfully vile."[10]

Some of Clarke's most convincing arguments and most eloquent passages describe man's plunge from paradise to perdition.

> From simple desire irregularly exercised, sprang the loss of Eden, loss of holiness, loss of God, and loss of happiness. By the envy of the devil sin entered . . . and death by sin; and with them innumerable evils . . . that have turned the paradise of God into a howling wilderness, driven peace from the earth, filled the body with the seeds of disease and death and the soul with the seeds of corruption and perdition.[11]

Thus every man is enslaved to sin, sinning against his own best interests even when he knows better, becoming a desperate thief robbing himself. There seems no end to the viciousness of sinful man; and "were it not for the restraining grace of God," says Clarke, "man would go on destroying his fellow til the last villain would be found standing alone on earth, and the devil the only person left to bury him."[12]

## 5. *Holiness Is Provided by Christ's Atonement*

To restore the image of God to man, which was forfeited in the Fall, is the aim of the gracious atonement of Christ. "Now this perfection is the restoration of man to the state of holiness . . . by creating him anew in Christ Jesus, and restoring him to that image . . . of God which he had lost."[13]

This possibility for sinful man is offered only through Christ's atonement which comes by no worthiness of our own but through Christ. Nothing less than Christ's sacrifice could rescue us. "Sin must be an inconceiveable evil, and possess an indescribeable malignity," proclaimed Clarke, "when it required no less a sacrifice than that offered by God manifested in the flesh."[14]

Clarke urged upon holiness seekers the fact that this blessing was by grace alone. It could not be attained by suffering or by death. Neither could it come by orthodoxy or good works. "Honesty, justice, integrity, and a strictly religious conduct, are all excellent, and are indispensable in the Christian character," Clarke declared. "But they are not the blood of atonement—the purifying influences of the Holy Ghost; nor can they be their substitutes."[15]

All the benefits of pardon, holiness, and heaven come from the atonement of Christ. "He was man that he might have blood to shed; and God, that when shed, it might be of infinite value."[16]

### 6. *Holiness Is Available in This Life*

Then, as now, there were many who thought that holy living was impossible. Even the Westminster Creed taught that men would sin every day in word, thought, and deed. Somehow in the hour and article of death, cleansing from sin was to occur. Adam Clarke did not hesitate to challenge this doctrine. He declared that to make death a more powerful savior than Christ was not only absurd but blasphemous.

Toward the Roman doctrine of purity through penal suffering in purgatory Clarke also directed salvos of scripture and logic. He declared that not one syllable of the Bible supported such a doctrine. Of both these doctrines he said, "In the whole Bible there is not one intimation that sin shall be destroyed in either the article of death, or in the other world. . . . *Here* we are to wash our robes, and make them white in the blood of the Lamb."[17]

Clarke was astonished that any student of the Bible should tell us "that we cannot be saved from all sin in this life. . . . So far as the trumpet gives this vile sound, it has not the authority of God's command."[18]

Today, of course, sanctification by death or purgatory would not be the antagonists of entire sanctification as much as other notions. One of the primary opponents is deterministic psychology (typified by B. F. Skinner), which says that man is not free and is shoved around by environmental forces he is not even aware of. This is a sort of Bezan Calvinism without a vertical dimension. Another discreditor which is Pelagianism without a vertical dimension is the humanistic movement which says man isn't sinful anyway. So why fix him if he isn't broken?

### 7. *Sanctification Is a Second Definite Work of Grace*

Clarke explained that holiness is produced by the Holy Spirit. Since that "Spirit is not an inmate of the heart till the soul is justified. . . . Justification . . . must precede sanctification."[19]

In another sermon he cited the "two grand doctrines of salvation," justification and sanctification. He showed that they are separate, and that a person does not automatically proceed to holiness just because he has been pardoned. The believer must seek sanctification on purpose, for "pardon of sin, as an act of God's mercy, does not imply the purification of the soul: the first removes the guilt, the second takes away the disposition that led to . . . transgression."[20] "The first of these great works is usually attributed to the shedding of Christ's blood . . . the second to the infusion of his Spirit."[21]

## 8. *Sanctification Is Received Instantaneously by Faith*

"In no part of Scripture are we to seek remission of sins *seriatim;* one now, another then, and so on," Clarke proclaimed. "Neither in any part are we directed to seek holiness *gradatim*. We are to come to God for an instantaneous and complete purification from all sin. . . . Neither *seriatim* pardon, nor *gradatim* purification exists in the Bible."[22]

Clarke was emphatic on this point. Growth may and must come after sanctification, but neither growth, suffering, good works, or death can produce it. In his sermon, "Genuine Happiness the Privilege of the Christian in This Life," Clarke declared that to every believer holiness is

offered in the present moment [and] . . . may in that moment be received. For as the work of cleansing and renewing the heart is the work of God, his almighty power can perform it in a moment, in the twinkling of an eye. And as it is at this moment our duty to love God with all our hearts, and we cannot do this til he cleanse our hearts, consequently he is ready to do it this moment. . . . This moment therefore we may be emptied of sin, filled with holiness, and become truly happy.[23]

He closed the sermon, "Love to God and Man" with a yearning appeal to his hearers to seek perfection instantaneously by faith. "Can he ever be more willing to cleanse our hearts from all unrighteousness than he is now? . . . Where is the faith to receive Him? . . ."

> *Faith, mighty Faith, the promise sees,*
>     *and looks to that alone;*
> *Laughs at impossibilities,*
>     *and cries it shall be done.*[24]

### 9. *Sanctification Is Wrought by the Holy Spirit, and to That Work the Spirit Witnesses*

It is nearly impossible to overstate the emphasis Clarke put on the work of the Holy Spirit. He hardly ever mentioned sanctification without saying that it is wrought by the Spirit.

Several times he appropriately reminded his hearers that the Spirit which indwells the holy is Christ's Spirit. "This very Spirit comes through Christ, and is the gift of Christ."[25]

Clarke strongly emphasized the Holy Spirit in conversion. Here the believer is given the Holy Ghost, the Spirit becomes an "inmate" of the heart and is even said to "indwell" the believer. In sanctification, however, the believer is "baptized with a greater effusion of the Holy Ghost,"[26] who washes away all sin.

Only three times in the 60 sermons did Clarke use the term "baptize" in reference to the Spirit's work. In addition to the instance quoted in the preceding paragraph, he closed one sermon with these words: "Go now to Christ, that he may purge your conscience from dead works, baptize you with the spirit of holiness, guide you by his counsel, and at last receive you into his glory."[27] He also referred to the baptism of the Spirit at Pentecost but did not relate it there to the experience of sanctification in any direct way.

A word that he seemed to prefer is "effusion." This word can be thought of as relating to baptism in an oblique manner, since one of its meanings is to pour out a liquid. It also means an unrestrained, freely flowing expression of words or feelings. Thus, in sanctification the Holy Spirit is poured out in His fullness.

Occasionally Clarke described the purifying and filling work of the Spirit as an "infusion" of the Holy Spirit.

But his most frequent term was "inspiration." Again and again he urged the people to seek cleansing through the "inspiration" of the Holy Ghost. There was a special reason for the choice of this rather vague term. Many if not most of Clarke's eager hearers had been catechized in the Anglican church. They knew its creed and memorized its rituals. The phrase "inspiration of the Holy Ghost" comes directly from the Anglican liturgy; it is part of the Collect for the Communion Service which goes this way:

> Almighty God, unto whom all hearts be open, all desires known, and from whom no secrets are hid: Cleanse the thoughts of our hearts by the inspiration of the Holy Spirit, that we may perfectly love thee, and worthily magnify thy holy name, through Christ our Lord. Amen.[28]

Clarke frequently used this collect intact or nearly so. When he did so, he was using something which many of his hearers had memorized and heard since childhood. Then too, the Wesleyans always claimed that their distinctive doctrine had always been in the creeds and, of course, in the Bible. They were not inventing something new, and this is a case in point.

According to Clarke, the sanctifying of the heart is the Holy Spirit's specialty. He preached on Isa. 1:18 to that effect:

> How is it that a nature so impure as ours can be purified from all unrighteousness? Why, by the Almighty Spirit. . . . that Spirit is called the Holy Spirit because his office is to produce holiness in the nature of man. He pervades that nature—purifies and refines, and sublimes it to himself. He is given through the blood of the covenant for this very purpose. He comes to accomplish this great end . . . [so we can be] justified freely, and sanctified wholly.[29]

The Spirit purifies, indwells, and fills the consecrated heart, Clarke believed. The heart was filled with all the

125

fullness of God, "emptied of sin . . . and filled with humility, meekness, gentleness, goodness, justice, holiness, mercy, truth, and love to God and man."[30] "The heart in which Christ constantly dwells, he completely fills and holiness becometh his house forever."[31]

In a unique illustration from the world of the graphic arts Clarke noted that the work of the sanctifying Spirit is to restore the image of God to man's being. "In the act of justification when the Spirit of God, the Spirit of holiness, is given to bear witness with our spirits . . . all the outlines of the divine image are drawn upon the soul; and it is the work of the Holy Spirit, in our sanctification, to touch off and fill up all those outlines, till every feature of the divine image is . . . perfected."[32]

To this glorious work the Holy Spirit gives a witness that goes beyond reason, logic, and science. It is impossible, said Clarke, that one should have all these wondrous works done in his inmost being and not know about it. The witness of the Spirit, the assurance of acceptance by God was a frequent theme of Clarke and the early Wesleyans in general.

### 10. *In Sanctification the Heart Is Cleansed from the Carnal Nature, Delivered from All Sin*

While many have looked to the "second blessing" for power for service and nearly ignore cleansing, Adam Clarke put great emphasis on cleansing and little on power. Perhaps to him there was much more miracle in cleansing than empowering.

He had a desperately serious view of the wickedness of the carnal nature. It causes man to commit all kinds of sins, for under its sway, "man, not satisfied with destroying his fellows . . . destroys also himself—makes his own life wretched, shortens his days, and ruins his own soul! His conduct, therefore, is not only unholy, it is unnatural. Reason, therefore, can be no director of his ways. . . . He even sins against his own convictions. . . . He resolves against it and is yet overcome."[33]

Thus, every person, even the converted, "carries in himself naturally a foeman's heart; and hence disputes, contentions, strifes, variance, emulations, hatred, malice, battery, private murders, and public wars."[34] Clarke therefore zealously warned the believers in a London congregation, "The seed of the serpent must not remain in your soul. . . . Sin will be continued. If we go not to God to have the evil principle of sin taken away from our hearts . . . we shall soon incur a new debt . . . and be deeply guilty before God."[35]

The answer to the sin problem is found in God, for "as far as sin has reached, so far can God's infinite mercy go; as wide as it has extended, so far can this infinite mercy extend itself: however great my sins have been, this mercy is infinitely without and above all their guilt; however deep my defilement may have been, I can see, that the infinitely penetrating holiness and purity of God goes deeper than all this. What need I more?"[36]

"What then is this complete sanctification?" Clarke asked. Then, answering his own question, he declared, "It is the cleansing of the blood that has not been cleansed—it is the washing of the soul of a true believer from the remains of sin—it is the making one who is already a child of God, more holy."[37] "The Holy Spirit, the Spirit of burning, destroys the pollution of the heart,"[38] and "the carnal mind [is] totally destroyed and the whole image of God restamped upon the soul."[39] This "certainly points out a *deliverance from all sin* . . . and if this be fulfilled in man surely sin shall be eradicated from the soul,"[40] for "the sanctifying Spirit . . . condemns to utter destruction the

127

whole of the carnal mind";[41] and for those who humbly seek Him, the Spirit brings "the purification of their hearts from all evil tempers, passions, and appetites; so that they can love God with all their hearts, and worthily magnify his name, and love their neighbor as themselves."[42]

To Clarke holiness was what really mattered. When convicted of his own need of it, he said, "I regarded nothing, not even life itself, in comparison with having my heart cleansed from all sin, and began to seek it with full purpose of soul."[43]

## 11. *Holiness Is Not Optional*

Clarke was not one to flippantly assert, "Holiness or hell." He believed that the seeker of holiness, whether or not he was a possessor, would be saved. In those days people were quick to seek the blessing, but slow to profess it. Clarke, nevertheless, was not reluctant to use Heb. 12:14, "Follow peace with all men, and holiness, without which no man shall see the Lord." He sometimes made a point of this: "Unless the soul in the day of the Lord be found saved from all power, guilt, and contamination of sin, it cannot inherit an eternal state of blessedness."[44] He sometimes said that justification exempted one from the punishment of hell, but sanctification prepared one to see God. "Without justification . . . it [the soul] must perish; without sanctification it cannot see God."[45] Further, an unholy man cannot enter heaven; and if he did, he wouldn't like it. He's not suited to it. "The nature of the resident must be suited to the place of residence. The fishes live not in the elms, and cattle browse not in the depths of the sea. Hell is for demons and wicked men; heaven, for holy angels, and the spirits of just men made perfect."[46]

## 12. *Holiness Is Necessary for Successful Christian Living*

Though the justified man must not sin, else he cease to be justified, the presence of the unsanctified carnal nature means trouble ahead. It is a contagion and "the grand hidden cause of transgression."[47] For the Christian with a carnal heart *obedience* soon becomes a chore, and after a while may likely be ignored. "The carnal mind is enmity against God, and to it every sacred duty is irksome, and every heavenly virtue hateful but . . . when the carnal mind is destroyed, then the enmity is destroyed, and obedience is delightful."[48] The sanctified Christian "lays out his life before God, spends it for God, and can be a confessor or martyr, rather than defile his conscience and grieve the Spirit of God."[49]

If the "seed of the serpent" is allowed to nestle in the Christian's heart, *perseverance* will be as rare as the "black swan." The Christian must be cleansed and remain clean. "Hence the necessity of abiding in a state of purity; without this there is no hope of perseverance."[50]

The will of God for man is a life of holiness. God declares "complete redemption of the man, putting him in a state of salvation, preserving him in that state, enabling him to serve . . . through the whole course of his life; . . . constantly holy in heart,"[51] and "simply and constantly depending on a looking to Jesus . . . he receives continual supplies of enlightening and sanctifying grace."[52] Clarke added that without holiness "perseverance is a mere fable."[53]

With carnal mindedness within, *happiness* for the Christian will likely be as hard to achieve as putting a vapor in a grocery sack. "Misery was never known till sin entered into the world; and happiness can never be known by any man until sin be expelled from his soul."[54] Clarke continued even more bluntly, "No holiness, no happiness; and no plenary and permanent happiness without plenary and permanent holiness."[55]

The unholy tempers of unsanctified Christians plagued Clarke severely from time to time. Those of a bitter, censorious spirit he compared to a popular medicine caHed "The Holy Bitter." Clarke said that neither the medicine nor the people ever did any good.[56] The development of such tempers come from a carnal heart; and to prevent this, a Christian must come to God who will "purify his soul . . . so that no unholy temper, evil desire, or impure affection or passion, should either lodge or have any being within him."[57]

Adam Clarke, as a young preacher in the Norman Isles, was blessed with a number of those Christians who were makers of Procrustes' bed. You remember him: He was the host with just one odd-shaped bed. If a visitor was too tall, he just chopped enough of his legs off to make him fit. To these people who measured everyone by their own odd standards, Clarke preached on holiness for weeks. Finally revival came and Clarke said many got over the Procrustes complex. For these and other negative attitudes Clarke consistently recommended "the purification of their hearts from all evil tempers, passions and appetites; so that they can love God with all their hearts, and worthily magnify his name."[58]

When the sanctifying Spirit comes into the heart in His fullness, the fruit of the Spirit displaces the evil tempers and passions. Love, joy, peace, long-suffering, gentleness, goodness, faith, meekness, and temperance "spring up with energy and strength, and all produce their respective classes of effects which prove them to be of God."[59] Thus the prayer of the Collect for the Communion Service, so often quoted by Clarke, is answered and fulfilled as sanctified Christians perfectly love God and worthily magnify His name. But "without holiness no man can see God; and without practical holiness no man can please him."[60]

## 13. Continual Growth in Grace Must Follow Sanctification

Sanctification is not terminal or static. It is the beginning of growth, not the end. It is "when the soul is purified ... that it can properly grow in grace ... as a field may be expected to produce a good crop . . . when the thorns, thistles, briers, and noxious weeds . . . are grubbed out."[61]

Those who have received the blessing of holiness "must grow in it—have more of God's light and love, and power in them," Adam Clarke told the congregation at Stanhope Street Chapel, Liverpool, in August, 1832, the same month that he died. He continued, "If they do not grow in grace, they will lose their grace; for all the graces that God gives he gives more to increase."[62]

The food of the inner man is knowledge, love, peace, and holiness. And the Holy Spirit abiding in the heart supplies this nourishment.[63] The holy Christian will daily grow in grace because the grace he has received "enlarges his mental powers. The soul grows in capacity and the grace grows according to increasing powers. And it is by continual growth that what he has already received is preserved."[64] He becomes a branch in the True Vine. If he abides, he flourishes; if not, he withers.

Clarke explains more fully his doctrine of growing in grace in his sermon, "Experimental Religion and Its Fruits."

> They now have righteousness—they are made partakers of the divine nature. They have a righteous principle in every power of their souls, and in every affection and passion of their hearts. It is not enough

131

that they are *saved from sin,* but they must be *filled with righteousness.* To empty and to fill are distinct operations of the Spirit of God. He first casts out sin; this he can do in a moment, in the twinkling of an eye; but the filling with righteousness is a progressive work, for the man is to increase more and more in KNOWL-EDGE; and as his increase in love depends on his increase in knowledge, and knowledge must be, from its very nature, gradually received; hence his growth in grace is gradual. In a moment he may be emptied of sin, and wherever evil was, there will a seed of righteousness be deposited; but that seed will require time to vegetate and grow; and as these seeds grow, so the powers of the soul expand; and in this way the immortal spirit may grow in holiness and excellence to all eternity. Being emptied of all sin is a small matter, when compared with being filled with God, or with all the fruits of righteousness.[65]

## 14. *Holiness of Heart Results in Christian Service*

Clarke took to task those Christians who "because they know they cannot be saved by their good works . . . are contented to have no good works at all."[66] To him the person who loves God with all his heart will "serve him with all his strength . . . love their neighbor as themselves . . . [and] live to get good from God, that they may do good to man."[67]

The ways that the sanctified are to serve are many, as we shall see in the next chapter.

## 15. *The Evidence of Holiness Is Love*

The assurance of the Spirit witnessing within is reinforced by the witness of the fruit of the Spirit in daily life. The principal fruit is *love*—love to God and love to others. The primary observable evidence is love—not code keeping, not ceremony, not self-righteousness, not legalism, but love.

## 16. *Holiness Should Be Preached Repeatedly and Often*

By his own modeling Adam Clarke showed us his belief in preaching holiness repeatedly and often. Truly he was a man of one message. He knew that many clergymen did not preach much on holiness. It was not a popular theme in many corners of Christendom. Clarke thought that it lacked popularity in some places because the "attainment of inward holiness is attended with so much self-denial, mortification, and taking up the cross, and [was] . . . so little experienced . . . that . . . the subject is left out of the pulpit."[68]

Yet Clarke felt that preaching holiness was pivotal and crucial for Methodism. In speaking to a Liverpool congregation that he had preached to 50 years before, and now on the eve of his own death, he said,

> I am fully satisfied of this . . . that while Methodists preach these truths [holiness was his subject] and in this order and way, it is impossible, in any nation of the world where the doctrine is preached, that the people can lose their religion; or that it can ever be said, that the revival of religion, once among the Methodists, has ceased.[69]

The preaching of holiness, Clarke believed, should not leave the people wondering about how to get it. In one of his sermons he gave 12 guidelines for entering into the experience.

1. Thou also art a subject of that mighty working of the corruption that is in the world through lust, or the principle of irregular and unholy desire.
2. Pray to God deeply to convince thee of thy fallen state, and to give thee true repentance.
3. Pray to God earnestly, that thou mayest never rest til thou hast a clear sense of thy acceptance with God, through the Son of his love.
4. As he convinced thee that thou hadst a guilty con-

133

science, and didst need pardon, pray to him that he may convince thee that thou hast a fallen nature—also an evil heart—a spirit that lusteth to envy—and that it must be regenerated and purified from all unrighteousness.

5. Seek this blessing with thy whole soul—in all things—in all means—in all times; never lose sight of thy necessity, and of God's ability to save.

6. Read the exceeding great and invaluable promises relative to this point; they are numerous, both in the Old and New Testaments.

7. Fear not to take the fullest view of inbred sin—beg of God to lead thee by his Spirit into every chamber of the house of imagery.

8. Having seen thy own heart, abhor thyself. Thou hast already received redemption in his blood, the forgiveness of sins; but feel, deeply feel, that thou must have the "very thoughts of thy heart cleansed by the inspiration of his Holy Spirit." Without this, thou canst not safely rest.

9. While seeking this salvation, let no sin, however refined in appearance, have any dominion over thee; beware of indulging any easily-besetting sin; abstain from every appearance of evil.

10. Strongly exercise the faith thou hast already. It is as much thy duty to strive to *believe*, as it is to strive to pray.

11. Do not give way to discouragement. He who hath promised to come will surely come.

12. See that thou bring forth the fruits of that faith and love which thou already hast; and in the spirit of loving obedience, according to thy present means of grace, expect that fulness of God which he has promised. Nothing can withstand the conquering blood of Jesus; nothing, the sovereign energy of his Almighty Spirit. He will shortly say, "Be clean;" and thou shalt be clean.[70]

# 10

# Personal Religion
# and Social Concern

"Oh, Mother, look. . . . Daddy's done it again."

Mary Clarke hurried to the window where her son Joseph stood pointing. She looked down the street. "I'm afraid you're right, son, I'm afraid you're right."

The sight that greeted her eyes was Rev. Adam Clarke striding briskly up the street toward their home. His prematurely gray hair bounced slightly in the breeze. He was dressed in the garb of an English country gentleman . . . blue coat, gray breeches, vest, and hat. As he walked through the ubiquitous British mist, he carefully stepped around the occasional mud puddles which pocked the street, for Adam Clarke, A.M., LL.D., was barefoot.

Adam Clarke,
> President of the Methodist Conference
> Member of the Royal Asiatic Society
> Fellow of the Antiquarian Society
> Subcommissioner of Public Records for the
> Crown
> President of the Philological Society
> Member of the Royal Irish Academy

Librarian of the Surrey Institute
Leader in the British and Foreign Bible Society
Fellow of the Geological Society, London
Member of the Eclectic Society of London
Author of some of the most learned works in
    existence
Master of 20 languages

was walking down a public street dressed in style from the ankles up. A barefoot dignitary he was. As he entered the door of his home, he was greeted by Mary his wife. "Addy," she said with only a hint of reproach in her voice, "you've given your shoes away again. Are you sure—"

"He was a destitute creature, Mary. Forced out of his home, he was. Not really able to work. I gave him one of John Wesley's tracts, too—although I doubt if he could read it. He'll be at the Methodist chapel on Sunday, I think."

"Adam, I thought you were going to bring 10 pounds of flour and 10 pounds of potatoes. You only have half that here."

"Well, Mary, this doleful old crippled woman was just ahead of me at the market. She was spending her last penny for a potato—she was buying one potato, Mary— one potato. I told the chap to give her five pounds. So I didn't have enough money left to get all you ordered after that; besides, I had already bought this little booklet at the press. I should have taken more money with me."

"I should have sent one of the children. That's what I'll do next time, I will."

"The opportunity of making happy is more scarce than we imagine. The punishment of missing it is never to meet with it again," Adam replied.

"You're right, Addy; but if anyone could find it again, it would be you—and that's alright with me; you know that, don't you?"[1]

136

**Millbrook, the residence of Clarke 1815-20. A farm estate near Liverpool.**

In this vignette we get a glance at the real Adam Clarke—a man of great learning, leadership, and honors, yet so touched by the needs of the poor that he would give away his own shoes on the spot. It was always a risk for Mary to send him to market, because there was a good chance he would give the shopping money away before he got there. He was no rich man giving from the largess of his abundance—he was a Methodist preacher.

James Everett said that when it came to such acts of generosity, Clarke's heart often stole a march on his judgment.[2] But to Clarke a holy heart was automatically and constantly being expressed in acts of concern. He told the congregation in Great Queen Street Chapel, London, that "when the carnal mind is destroyed, then that man . . . feels for . . . his brother, takes him in the arms of love and

. . . is ready to spend and be spent for his present and eternal welfare."[3]

Adam Clarke modeled the ideal combination of personal religion and social concern. He shared with Wesley the idea that the Church should change the world on the basis of Christian principles. Clarke was generous to a fault in his personal life, worked incessantly to help others, and also lent his influence and support to the people and organizations which were trying to solve the most crucial concerns. The Sunday School, missions, charity schools, hospitals, child labor laws, the antislavery movement, and relief for the poor were given strong support by Clarke and many other Methodists. It may well be that the world has never seen a better marriage of personal religion and social concern than that modeled by John Wesley, Adam Clarke, and the early Methodists. It is a marriage worth renewing.

Wherever Clarke went, he could not keep from reaching out to the spiritual and physical needs of the people around him. In 1815 he left the whirlwind of a London ministry because of poor health and a need to concentrate on the Commentary. He moved to a farm called Millbrook in a quiet countryside several miles from Liverpool. But the quiet didn't last long.

Clarke found that his neighbors in the region were Catholics or entirely unchurched. Most could not read. They were very poor. Adam and his wife and daughters began to try to change all that. His daughters taught many of the adults to read, distributed Bibles, taught classes, gave food to the poor, and made clothes for children. Together the Clarkes organized a Sunday School of 40 children. Adam then, at his own expense, built a chapel that would seat 300. The Sunday School scholars were taught to read, taught the church liturgy and simple religious songs. Through these compassionate ministries many were won to God, and a small Methodist society was organized. It started with the children who "were noticed and instructed; and the parents, persuaded by their little ones, came—at first, from curiosity, to listen—from this to inquire—to weep and to pray."[4]

Several years later, when Clarke had returned to the London area, an epidemic swept the city, and the Clarkes turned part of their large house into an infirmary for the poor. They started a Sunday School on their property here too. A depression also hit England during the 1820s, and during that time the Clarke family cut their own table rations dangerously low in order to help feed the hungry in their neighborhood.

Though Clarke was constantly involved in curing social ills, he did not let them dominate his pulpit ministry (as we saw in Chapter 3). In the pulpit Clarke was dealing with the most vital needs of man—spiritual needs. Even in his frequent fund raisers for hospitals or charity schools he nearly always preached on full salvation; then, for a few minutes at the end of the address, he would present the "cause."

Clarke felt that when preachers brought their personal politics into the pulpit that the church was split and unedified, and sinners were left unconverted. Clarke lived during the American Revolution, the French Revolution, and the Napoleonic Wars. These events sent shudders to the political soul of England. In near political panic many clergymen tried to solve the world problems in the pulpit with little positive results. When asked how he handled these issues during the French Revolution, Clarke answered that he preached on entire sanctification for the duration of the revolt.

Clarke told his congregations to be loyal to their government as an institution of God. He reminded them that under the British Constitution not even the king himself could abridge their rights. Through this period of political earthquakes which so shook England, he urged them not to get unwisely involved in civil commotions. He, however, felt free to preach and write against political corruption, the impressment of seamen, slavery, and war.

Let us examine briefly some of the social concerns which found a place in Clarke's life and preaching.

## 1. *Helping the Poor*

The social concern that received the most attention in the preserved sermons is the duty of every Christian to help the poor. This was taken for granted with those early Methodists. To the weekly class meetings every Methodist was to bring an offering to the poor. Even if the member himself was poor, he was urged to participate because there was always someone more destitute than he. It was felt that the poor man who is not willing to help those worse off than himself will never give even when he prospers. "Sometimes he feels he might give more to the poor, and do more good with what he has, but he will soon find a reason to excuse himself even from this."[5] If we love God and man, it will show. "Whatever love we may pretend to mankind, if we are not charitable and benevolent, we give the lie to our profession," Clarke declared. "If . . . we have not the love of God in us; if we shut up our bowels against the poor, we shut Christ out of our hearts, and ourselves out of heaven."[6]

"Draw out your soul to the hungry," Clarke challenged a Manchester congregation; "be . . . every poor man's friend; and do not starve your own souls, and pamper your flesh, lest you hear to your eternal dismay, 'Remember that you in your lifetime received your good things.'"[7] He called upon those who had sharecroppers and renters on their lands not to foreclose on them just because they could. He urged them instead to discover the blessing of forgiving debts. "Learn . . . to give and forgive . . ." he said, "and never turn away thy face from any poor man; so the face of God shall never be turned away from thee."[8] Those who rejected this were warned, in the same sermon in a dramatic aside, "O monster ingratitude! Scandal to human nature, and reproach to God! Go, and, if thou canst, hide thyself—even in hell—from the face of the Lord!"[9]

Clarke also opposed those twin evils which keep the poor poor—usury and credit buying. He called upon his hearers to do without rather than buy on credit. As for anyone who charged a poor man over 5 percent interest, Clarke recommended that the names of these hardhearted villains be posted at every major intersection. After this exposure, he suggested, they be deported to live with the savages of New Zealand.

When Clarke in his fourth year of ministerial work was sent to the Norman Isles to pastor, he found many of the gentry in his congregation. But Clarke was so interested in the poor of the islands that the gentry gradually stopped coming and left him with none but the poor, which he called "the best friends of my God."[10] But while the poor languished, those better off continued in celebration which Clarke thought extravagant.

A local preacher who worked with Clarke had to put his children to bed in the daytime to keep them from freezing and starving. He had no food and no coal and no money to buy either. At the very moment this was happening, an "illumination" festival was going on. Clarke's reaction was: "Had a portion of the cash wasted . . . been appropriated to the relief of this distressed good man, how gladly would the first scribe in heaven have registered it in the annals of eternity!"[11]

Clarke's concern for the poor is poignantly portrayed

in this letter he wrote at the time of the festival just described.

> When I consider the suffering state of these *more righteous than I,* I can scarcely eat my morsel with contentment. If there is meaning in the expression, *"a bleeding heart,"* I do think I have it for the poor. My very soul seems to feel for the whole of them throughout the world, as my father, my sister, my mother and my brethren! . . . Forgive me if, in dilating on the subject which oppresses my heart, but I have forgotten to write about the full salvation you inquired after; but is it not found in the bowels of Christ? and were not these exercised in continual outgoings for the poor? He lived for the poor; he died for the poor; and blessed is he who *remembereth* the poor, even supposing he is not able to help them. I know I feel the spirit and power of Christ, in proportion as I feel love, modified into compassion and pity.[12]

Clarke did more than merely wish the poor could do better. About two years after the letter cited above was written, Clarke was assigned to Bristol. There he and John Wesley organized the first Stranger's Friend Society. The next year he organized another in Dublin. Within four years he had organized Stranger's Friend Societies in Liverpool, Manchester, and London. From there they spread all over England. And when Clarke died in 1832, most cities of any size had a Stranger's Friend Society, usually operated by Methodists, but many persons of goodwill who were not Methodists gave to this great ministry. It is hard to estimate how far this went in helping England avoid the uprisings of the poor like France experienced. It may very well be that this and other reforms influenced by the Methodist revival saved England from a bloody revolution.

The Stranger's Friend Society was made up of volunteers who took as their motto "As ye are so shall the stranger be." In order to try to make this equality a reality, each member pledged to give a weekly contribution for the relief of the poor. No Methodist could receive help from this society, for the Methodists had their own adequate sources of relief. This was an outreach ministry. Any destitute person, regardless of race, religion, or political party, could receive emergency aid.

For the man with the "bleeding heart" for the poor the success of this plan was immensely gratifying. In 1821 he wrote to the national treasurer of the Stranger's Friend Society, "Had I been the means of doing no other good among men than being the original institutor of the Stranger's Friend Society, I should have reason to thank God that I was ever born, and to praise him for ever that he had thus condescended to use me."[13]

Two other organizations which provided medical aid for the poor in London received significant fund-raising support from Adam Clarke. They were the Royal Humane Society and a Methodist concern called the Ladies Lying-in Hospital; the latter was an institution for destitute pregnant women. London was in the process of becoming an industrialized city. New people daily moved into the already overcrowded city. Among this teeming mass of humanity were many mothers-to-be who were alone, penniless, and hopeless. The Methodist Lying-in Hospital cared for up to 300 such women per year. They were provided with food, clothes, a place to stay, a place to give birth, rehabilitation (when required and accepted), and of course religious instruction. To a London congregation Adam Clarke said, "It ought to yield great satisfaction to our minds, that God is pleased to make us instruments in bringing poor women of this kind through their dangers and difficulties."[14]

Clarke considered riches a hazard to the Christian's health. He regularly warned and urged his hearers lest "they might possess their temporal things, so as to lose eternal things."[15] Those who garner much silver and gold are in the gravest danger, because "not one in 100,000 who has these . . . does not treat them as gods, by building all his hopes on them and seeking all his happiness from them!"[16] This risk comes not only to the rich but to those who merely yearn to be monied. "The ardent pursuit of riches is as destructive," Clarke warns, "as the possession of them is dangerous."[17] Further, if God does prosper a person, God is putting the poor in his trust and expects the prospered one to minister to the poor and not his own pleasures.[18]

I sometimes wonder how the share of the modern church's budget which goes to the poor compares with the share of the budget the early Wesleyans gave to the poor.

## 2. *Slavery*

Among the most vigorous opponents of slavery were the Methodists; and among the Methodists who opposed slavery most vigorously was Adam Clarke. He and Samuel Bradburn led a sugar boycott in which they "induced many to leave off that drug. A drug composed of the slave dealer's sin and the slaves' misery."[19] They published a pamphlet called "An Address to the People Called Methodist Concerning the Evil of Encouraging the Slave Trade." They hoped to reduce the demand for West Indian sugar, and slaves to grow it, as well as publicizing the evil of slavery.

Clarke opposed slavery in every way he could. A pro-slavery man engaged Clarke in parlor conversation, and Clarke told him that slavery was a scandal to the British Empire. The slaves' "liberty is not ours. It belongs to God and themselves. The highest angel of God cannot claim a control over it. Our legislature sanctioned it in the beginning . . . and now, after being forced to acknowledge our iniquity, we hesitate to undo our wicked acts!"[20]

"But would you advise that they all be immediately emancipated?"

"Most certainly," Clarke answered.

"Then they would knock us all on the head."

"Possibly," Clarke answered, "and therefore take care of your heads. . . . Their liberty is their own, and you have no right to it—not for one moment."[21] On another occasion he said, "I here register my testimonies against the un-principled, inhuman, Antichristian, and diabolical slave trade, with all its authors, promoters, abettors, and sacri-legious gains; as well as against the great devil, the father of it and them."[22] This came from a man whose brother, Tracy Clarke, was, for a time, a doctor on a slave ship.

At the Conference of 1830 Clarke and others passed a strong resolution against slavery. The action called for a drive to obtain more than a million petitions to put before parliament. Clarke wrote that day to Mr. and Mrs. For-shaw, abolitionist colleagues of his, and to Wilberforce:

> You will see from the preceding resolutions what the Methodist ministers have done as a body, which is to be followed by petitions from every society and con-gregation in the united kingdom, separately signed; and these will bring before the two houses of the legis-lature, at least one million of names of honest men, who are determined to use their preponderating in-fluence in all the counties of England, to petition for the speedy and total abolition of colonial slavery!
>
> There is no time now for trifling, or half measures. We have put our hands to the work, and by the help of God we will do it with our might![23]

Wilberforce wrote back:

> My Dear Dr. Clarke,—For you will permit me, I trust, to use the language of friendly regard, since I can truly assure you it is warranted abundantly by the undissembled feelings of my heart. I return you many thanks for your kind and highly gratifying communica-tion. The "resolutions" are truly excellent; and I rejoice to hear that the cause of the poor slaves will be so

zealously pleaded for by your numerous congregations.[24]

But Clarke and the Methodists were not satisfied merely to seek the political freedom of the slaves. They wanted to save their souls. Four months before he died, Adam Clarke preached in Great Queen Street Chapel, London, on the anniversary of the Wesleyan Missionary Society. It was a fund raiser, and Clarke preached on "God's Love in Jesus Christ" from 1 John 3:1-2. In the conclusion of the sermon he cited the heroic work of the Wesleyan missionaries. One of the items he stressed was that in the West Indies colonies alone there were 24,499 slaves who were Methodists.[25]

### 3. *The Child Labor Laws*

During Clarke's lifetime England was developing as a major textiles producer. Factories sprang up everywhere. The live-in labor force was largely children. Factory owners would offer parents a certain amount of money for the use of their children. Most families had more mouths than they could feed, and so bargains apparently were quite easily struck. The child then would go to live at the factory. He or she would work 12-14 hours per day, six days per week. Being religious, the factory owners usually gave them Sunday off.

Adam Clarke was one who supported remedial labor laws. He circulated papers urging the passage of a bill to limit child labor. Further, he arranged a dinner with several factory owners who had "in their employ twelve or fifteen thousand children." He spoke of the bill and its "most benevolent principle." He had high hopes that these men would themselves support the bill, get it passed, and willingly comply. But to his astonishment they all opposed him to a man—even those described as "intelligent, pious, and humane." Their answer to Clarke sounds marvelously

146

like the double-talk of greed and power which every generation has to put up with. They opposed the bill on these
grounds.

> They spoke of it as a measure fraught with the
> deepest and most extensive mischief;—a measure,
> which had for its object the total abolition of Sunday-
> school, religious instruction, the Sabbath-day, all
> Methodist and other such preaching; and which, if
> passed into a law, would be an antidote to all our reli-
> gious blessings, and a wide-wasting curse: that they
> were prepared to prove by the most incontrovertible
> evidence, that the health and morals of the children in
> the manufactories, were beyond all comparison better
> than those who were out of them; and that they grew
> into more effective men and women than others. They
> added, that the very idea of being visited by the Gov-
> ernment inspectors, was hateful to them.[26]

## 4. *Education*

Few people believed in education more than Adam
Clarke. He knew that learning unlocked the treasure house
of the great ideas of the universe. He knew that learning
to read the Bible unlocked the gates of heaven. He was an
energetic supporter of the Sunday School, which came into
being about the time he started preaching. The Sunday
School's task then was first to teach the pupil to read and
write, then to help him or her read the Scriptures. Clarke
extolled the virtues of the teachers in the Sunday Schools.
He spoke as a guest speaker without pay to help establish
or pay off the debt of a number of Sunday Schools and
charity schools. He loved children and felt as though no
sacrifice was too great to unlock their minds to the possi-
bilities of learning.

The unlearned children who most preyed upon his
mind were the urchins who roamed the hills of his native
Northern Ireland, untaught and uncared for. Much of the
area was served by no schools at all. He wanted the Meth-

147

odist Conference to do something about it, but he couldn't get any action—so he did it himself.

Because of his many honors and memberships in learned societies he knew many people of some wealth. Going to these non-Methodist sources, he raised enough money to build six schools and hire teachers and provide supplies for them. The report after a year in operation was 666 students in these six schools.

Clarke visited the schools several times before he died. Some of the most pathos-filled writings of Clarke are his journal descriptions of the pitiable urchins who first learned to write, pray, and read the Bible in the Irish schools of Adam Clarke.

### 5. *The Shetland Islands*

In 1822 Clarke was for the third time president of the conference. The conference heard a report on the need for religious instruction in the Shetland Islands, the northernmost part of Britain. Clarke's mother's family had come from the Hebrides, and he listened to the needs of these islanders with great interest. Adam "rose, urged on the Conference the duty of taking the work at once in hand and concluded by proposing that two missionaries should be thereupon appointed."[27] But there were some who said it wasn't financially possible. When it looked like the issue would be lost for lack of budget, Chairman Clarke said that he personally would see to it that the money was supplied. Upon this proposal the issue was passed, and John Raby and Samuel Dunn were appointed to start the work.

Clarke went to work raising the money and soon had several hundred pounds in hand and a trust of £30,000 (at that time about $150,000—a small fortune). Clarke visited the work in 1826 and again in 1828, taking with him large supplies of clothing, blankets, Bibles, and other goods. By 1828 six Methodist societies were operating, with about 1,300 members. One of Clarke's preserved sermons, "Apostolic Preaching," was delivered in Lerwick, Shetland. As usual it was a sermon on sanctification.

## 6. *War*

Adam Clarke was not a pacifist but he was against war. To a London congregation he said, "Now the fiend of war is laid: God has chained him down in his own hell. The sword is put into its scabbard; and with all my soul, I pray that the Almighty God may give it an eternal rust there: may it never be withdrawn!"[28]

Clarke was very loyal to the Crown, but he didn't hesitate to condemn an unjust war. "I believe the present murderous war has, on our side, been wrong from the beginning," he asserted. "We should never have engaged in it; there was not one political or moral reason why we should: it is the war of Pitt's ambition;—a crusade in behalf of popery. I have heard all the reasons that have been urged for its support; it has ruined Europe—has aggrandized our enemies—and is ruining us:—no sophistry can prove the contrary nor make it even plausible."[29]

## 7. *Tobacco*

It was not unusual to see children of eight years smoking pipes and cigars on the streets in Clarke's day. Even some Methodist preachers were addicted. Clarke's own parents used tobacco to the day of their deaths.

Adam was convinced that it was an unmixed evil. One of his first publications was a pamphlet against the use of tobacco. It had a long and fruitful life. One of the preachers at the conference in 1805 got up and told the conference, "My wife and I used tobacco for between 30 and 40 years. When I read Mr. Clarke's pamphlet I was convinced I should give it up. I did so and so did my wife. I then recommended it to the society . . . many of whom were addicted to it. All who read the pamphlet gave it up."[30]

Eventually it became a rule of the conference that no preacher could be admitted to "full connection" who used tobacco. There were some interesting happenings along the way. This interview occurred while Adam Clarke was the conference president. It was his duty to examine the ministerial candidates before the whole congregation and ordain them. Here is part of one such interview:

Dr. Clarke—"Do you use tobacco in any form, brother?"

Candidate—"A little, Sir."

Dr. C.—"You must give it up."

Cand.—"I use it for the sake of health, Sir."

Dr. C.—"Our rule is against it, and I cannot admit you, unless you will give it up."

Cand.—"Well, Sir, I will try to give it up."

Dr. C.—"An attempt will do nothing, unless persevered in."

Cand.—"I think it hard, Sir, where health requires it."

Dr. C.—"Our rule knows no exceptions; and I would not, in the situation in which I am placed, admit my own father—no not an angel from heaven, without the pledge of total abandonment. You can take time to consider it; do nothing rashly; if, after you have thought upon it a day or two, or another year, you think you can conscientiously give the pledge, you can then be received."

Cand.—"Well, Sir, I feel inclined to relinquish it."

Dr. C.—"Do you solemnly promise it?"

Cand.—"I do, Sir."

Dr. C.—"Express yourself clearly, brother.—Am I to understand that you will bind yourself to give it up *now*—only for a short period, and be at liberty to resume it? There is no mental reservation, is there?"

Cand.—"I cannot say, Sir, what circumstances of health, etc., might occur to call for it; but I intend it at present."

Dr. C.—"On these terms, I will not receive you. You can make the experiment for twelve months; and then if you think you can subscribe to the requirement, you can come forward for full admission into the work."

Cand.—*Pausing—somewhat chagrined—and perceiving the case to deepen in serious effect,*—"Well, then, Sir, I solemnly promise to give it up."

Dr. C.—"For ever?"

Cand.—"Yes, by the help of God, not to resume it."[31]

Another interview on the same subject went this way:

Dr. C.—"Do you take tobacco in any form, brother?"

2nd Cand.—*(Somewhat pertly)* "I take a little snuff, Sir."

Dr. C.—"Give it up."

2nd Cand.—"I will give it up, Sir, if the Conference require me."

Dr. C.—"I am the Conference, Sir, while I am seated here, and I order you to give it up."

2nd Cand.—*A good deal toned down by the doctor's authoritative air, and handing out a small box, about the size of the first joint of his thumb*— "That serves me some months, Sir."

Dr. C.—"Hand it this way; as it is so *small,* it can be no great cross to give it up."[32]

Clarke was very active in support of many worthy causes. His work for the London Bible Society was remarkable. He was always seeking to meet the physical and spiritual needs of his fellowman; for, as he said, "Our Lord shows that the acts of kindness are to be done to any person in distress, of whatever nation, religion, or kindred he may be; and this kindness should be done to him that is near us, either in person, or in proxy, or by report."[33] Like a true Wesleyan, Clarke saw the world as his parish.

It would be unwise for today's Wesleyans to try to

exactly duplicate the work of Clarke and the early Methodists. Rather they should see the principle of the marriage between personal religion and compassionate concern for the welfare of the whole person. Being true to their heritage, they should bring the sanctified influence of the church to bear on the problems and forces that oppress and deprive people today. The sanctified life includes whatever service the times and human needs demand in the name of Christ.

# 11

# Clarke Counsels Today's Minister

A well-meaning friend of mine attended a "pastors' school" at a superchurch near Chicago. Inspired past goose bumps and almost into spasms, he returned to his own church of 98 members and tried to build before sundown a carbon copy of "Chicago Super." You know the rest—by midnight he had 98 puzzled members and by a week from Sunday a dozen missing members.

A minister could make the same kind of mistake trying to make his ministry an exact carbon copy of Adam Clarke's. Your sermon illustrations can be more appropriate to your times than his. Your own expository preaching (if you work at it) can suit the needs of your hearers better than a memorized rerun of Clarke's unique reason-exposition discourses. But with this caution heeded, it would do most of us a lot of good to sit down with Adam Clarke for a chat about ministers and ministry. If you could, you might hear some sage advice about the following.

### 1. *A God-called Ministry*

Adam Clarke recognized that the New Testament teaches that God calls teachers, evangelists, and apostles as well as preachers. He lamented that the Methodists had rolled all these gifts into one, "and a man must be either a *preacher* or nothing."[1] Like Clarke we should realize that God calls persons today to be teaching ministers, youth pastors, evangelists, music ministers, and so forth, as well as preaching pastors.

For Clarke the height of foolishness was to enter the ministry without a call. "He among us who is not convinced that he has an extraordinary call to the ministry will never seek for extraordinary help, will sink under discouragements and persecutions and . . . be . . . a slothful servant."[2] In his sermon "The High Commission" Clarke demands a called ministry because

> a man who does not feel that he carries on his heart an almost oppressive load of concern for a lost world will not, cannot go forth with that zeal, self-denial, and laborious exertion, requisite to save souls. And even this man, who is all fervour, and whose soul is wholly in the work, will not . . . be successful unless he have an extra-influence of the Holy Spirit with him.[3]

Clarke believed it was God's business to call whom He would. It was the church's business to examine and assign those who claimed to be called. He gives some guidelines to the church about these upon whom they should lay ordaining hands. They should be:

a. *Called of God.* "Without such a call he had better be a galley slave."[4] Pretended pastors have already troubled God's Church too much; these men "feed themselves, not the flock; men who are too proud to beg, and too lazy to work; who have neither grace nor gifts to plant the . . . cross on the devil's territories . . . and spoil him of his subjects."[5] They are "prophets who prefer hunting the hare or

154

the fox and pursuing the partridge and pheasant, to visiting the sick, and going after the . . . lost sheep."[6] "How can," Clarke wonders, "worldly minded, hireling, fox-hunting, and card-playing priests read Ezekiel 34:2 etc., without trembling to the centre of their souls?"[7]

    b. *Regenerated and filled with the Spirit of holiness.*

    c. *Persons with some natural abilities and aptitude for the work.* "To make a man a Christian minister who is unqualified for any function of civil life is sacrilege before God."[8] The one to ordain to the ministry is not that person "who has not intellect sufficient for a common trade."[9]

    d. *Persons who have gracious gifts,* for "if the grace of God do not communicate ministerial qualifications, no natural gifts, however splendid, can avail."[10]

    e. *Persons whose ministry bears fruit.* "How contemptible must that man appear . . . who boasts of his clerical education, his sacerdotal order, his legitimate authority to preach, administer the Christian sacraments, etc., while no soul is benefited by his ministry."[11]

    f. *Persons who cultivate their minds.* "A fool, or a blockhead, can never teach others the way of salvation. The highest abilities are not too great for a preacher of the gospel; nor is it possible that he can have too much human learning. But all is nothing unless he can bring the grace and Spirit of God into all his ministrations."[12]

    g. *Persons who can apply their knowledge to life.* Knowledge is useless unless applied practically to life.[13]

    h. *Persons who can admit their mistakes.* "The man who scarcely ever allows himself to be wrong is one of whom it may be safely said, 'He is seldom right.' It is possible for a man to mistake his own will for the will of God, and his own obstinancy for inflexible adherence to his duty."[14]

    i. *Persons who are touched by the afflicted and dying.*

j. *Persons who take no "barbarous pleasure" in expelling members from the church.*

k. *Persons who see themselves as "day laborers" in the harvest and not lords of it.*

l. *Persons who possess both prudence and zeal.*

m. *Persons who pray a lot.* "Go from your knees to the chapel. Get a renewal of your commission every time you go to preach. . . . Carry your authority to declare the gospel of Christ not in your hand, but in your heart."[15]

## 2. *Sermon Preparation*

Few preachers can follow Clarke's example of preaching without notes or manuscript. But we can learn from Clarke about thorough preparation. Clarke prepared so thoroughly that he could present a well-argued and organized sermon without notes. He did not enter the pulpit and just open his mouth. "I never dared to expect the Divine assistance and unction," Clarke said, "unless I had previously exercised my judgment and understanding as far as possible."[16]

Which of us today cannot profit from this modeling of Clarke: "I did not enter the pulpit or take my text, till I was satisfied I understood the subject and could properly explain and reason upon it."[17]

Clarke's wide range of reading, study, and observations brought variety and meaning to his preaching which one described as "new and uncommon . . . always interesting, and ever popular."[18] If the lack of these qualities plague a preacher's pulpit efforts, perhaps he or she can profit from Clarke's example of serious preparation. It may mean umpiring fewer church softball games, attending fewer socials, cutting down on committee meetings, and taking down the sign on the door which reads "Office" and replacing it with "Study," but the effort will likely be fruitful.

### 3. *A Lifelong Student*

Clarke was grieved by certain of his ministerial colleagues who were ignorant and proud of it. He urged the young preachers to make time for study. In a letter to a young preacher he wrote:

> You do well to cultivate your mind as far as you possibly can. You ought to do so, as a minister of the gospel, and as a man. I believe the intellect of Adam was created dependent on cultivation, for that perfection of which God had made it capable. I thank God, I have lived to some purpose in the Methodist connection having induced several preachers to acquire a knowledge of the Greek and Hebrew scriptures; and hope we shall, ere long, have not only a pious, but a learned and efficient ministry.[19]

As usual, Adam Clarke practiced what he preached in the matter of study and learning. He was a lifelong student. In his last sermon he said:

> Fifty years have now passed since I first came to this place preaching the unsearchable riches of Christ: then your preacher was a young boy in years, unskilled in experience, untaught in knowledge—but not wholly unlearned in the truth which maketh wise the simple. Since that time I have been always learning; I have studied my own heart, and there is yet work *there* to be done; I have been observing the ways and striving to know the love of God; in which is indeed a height to attain, a depth to penetrate, a breadth to understand, which increase in magnitude as we draw nearer to the fountain of light and glory. And *now,* my brethren, I come again before you; my hairs are now gray; yet I acknowledge it as my proudest boast, that Adam Clarke is still a *learner* at the feet of his Master.[20]

### 4. *Time Management*

Most ministers are overworked. There is no way for them to get caught up and stay that way. Therefore setting priorities and skillfully managing the days and hours is important. Adam Clarke said the key was to "keep pace with time and union with God."[21] It is not always easy to do both of these at once.

Clarke had remarkable success at this point. Part of his secret was organization. "Order is Heaven's first law," he explained. "The want of it is ruinous. I think how much I owe to it. Had it not been for this, I should have read little and written less."[22] It is probably true that Clarke read more books on horseback than some of us read in the study. He had a pocket library of several reference books that he carried in a briefcase wherever he went. He lost no time while riding in coaches or ferries—there was always study to be done. His son observed that "in everything he observed system, and conscientiously redeemed time: he gave himself no leisure, not even for an hour."[23] This observation may be a little extreme, for Clarke warned against overwork and other excesses.

Part of Clarke's time management plan is known. He arose at 4 a.m. in the summer and 5 a.m. in the winter. This gave him several hours in the study before the family gathered for breakfast and morning prayers at 8:00 or 8:30. He worked on various pastoral duties during the day. He rejected any and all invitations to the traditional afternoon tea. He said he added several years to his work life by so doing. He conducted family prayer again in the evening. He always went to bed exactly at 10 p.m. His vast library was kept in perfect order. Any book used was always replaced on the shelf before he left the study. Order and time management were his special skills. "Life, at longest, is but short, and every hour has work for itself," asserted Clarke, "therefore there is no time to spare; not one hour that we can afford to lose."[24]

## 5. *Pastoral Care*

Clarke was not a pastor who preached and then withdrew to his books. His heart was with his people, especially the sick. When his son Joseph became a vicar, Adam advised him to "read much, pray much, believe much. Visit the people from house to house. Take notice of the children; treat them lovingly."[25] In his sermon "Apostolic Preaching" Clarke declared: "A preacher who contents himself with merely his pulpit duties, or general catechetical work, is not likely to have a congregation truly spiritual. . . . Paul 'showed and taught publicly . . . from house to house.'"[26]

Clarke added that the people in most places are destroyed for lack of knowledge and that Paul, by explaining and teaching the gospel from house to house, was setting a timeless example for faithful pastors of all generations.

Clarke did not omit his own family from his pastoral ministrations. Who can match his twice daily prayer times with his family? In addition he creatively found time for the children. When he went on long journeys for the conference, he frequently took one of the older children with him. What influence for good must have enriched the lives of John, Joseph, and Mary Ann as they accompanied Adam on a two- or three-week tour of the churches. Further, when Clarke was away, he wrote letters to his children and, later, to his grandchildren. Perhaps his greatness or at least goodness shines most brightly in his letters to his family. To his daughter Mary Ann, now grown and married, he wrote a letter on her birthday which included this prayer:

> Sovereign of the heavens and of the earth, behold this my daughter on the anniversary of her birth day; I bring her especially before thee; fill her with thy light, life, and power; as in thee 'she lives, moves, and has her being,' so may she ever live to thee. Strengthen her, O thou Almighty—Instruct and counsel her; O thou Omniscient!—Be her prop, her stay; her shield, and her sword. Put all her enemies under her feet;—deck her

159

with glory and honour;—make her an example to her family,—a pattern of piety to her friends,—a solace to the poor,—and a teacher of wisdom to those who are ignorant and out of the way;—and on all her glory let there be a defence to preserve, and in every respect to render it efficient! By her may thy name ever be glorified; and in her may the most adorable Saviour ever 'see of the travail of his soul and be satisfied.' Amen, amen. So be it;—and let her heart hear and feel THY Amen, which is, so it shall be—Hallelujah.[27]

Such was his love and pastoral care of his own family.

## 6. *Hard Work*

Nothing demonstrates more the relationship between hard work and achievement than the life of Rev. Adam Clarke. With little opportunity and advantage he worked at the job. He mastered language study without a teacher; he learned to preach, to pray, to pastor. He studied science, history, and medicine. He preached to multitudes, led the Methodists, established schools and missions, and wrote volumes. His extant works fill some 15 small-print volumes, besides the 7,000-page *Commentary on the Bible*. His contributions and achievements as *either* preacher, leader, or writer would equal the lifework of most people.

He could not tolerate idleness, particularly from "religious loungers," as he called preachers who showed an aversion to hard work. He taught that Christians should never "be satisfied with doing less than is required."[28] To his son John he wrote, "Enter radically into everything you attempt to learn; and never, never be contented with superficial knowledge of anything."[29] The idler is next to the sabbath-breaker, Clarke believed; he who idles away his time on the six days is equally culpable, in the sight of God, as he who works on the seventh.

Clarke was not afraid to try. So often we may look at

the obstacles and give up without ever trying. Perhaps our greatest embarrassment at the Judgment will be the smallness of our *trying*. Adam Clarke coaches us to attempt great things in Christ's name.

# 12

# Adam Clarke's Legacy for Today

The late August sun pierced the London mists from time to time, mocking with dancing, gold-gilt shadows the faces of the mourning Methodists who stood with pierced hearts in the cemetery behind City Road Chapel. Or perhaps the sun was trying to bring some symbol of hope to these doleful men and women who had come to bury their patriarch who had lived like a saint, written like a scholar of scholars, and preached like an apostle.

On August 26, 1832, Adam Clarke had fulfilled one of his oft-remarked hopes—that his life and his work would end at the same time. He was on a preaching mission when cholera crushed the life out of his 72-year-old frame.

On August 5 he had delivered the keynote address at the conference in Liverpool. Then he left the conference early, telling his friends that he must return to London because cholera was waging a war on human life there. The Clarkes had turned part of their large home into a sick bay for cholera-stricken children. "I must get home," Clarke said; "my house will be full of children."[1]

He left Liverpool, traveling to Frome, where on the

14th of August he helped his son the vicar organize a new society for the relief of the poor. On August 19 he preached at Westbury, near Bristol. August 20 found him arriving at Bayswater, near London. On the 21st he called in the homes of one of his sons and two of his daughters who lived in the London area. He prayed with his children and grandchildren, giving each a patriarchal blessing. He even interrupted the nap of two of his grandchildren for the last "blessing and hug." He got home to Mary that night about 7:00.

He spent the next two days in letter writing and settling certain accounts. At the family worship, which occurred both morning and evening in the Clarke household, he invariably prayed in reference to the cholera plague that "each and all might be saved from its influence or [be] prepared for sudden death."

On Saturday, August 25, he opened the family prayer with "We thank thee, O heavenly Father, that we have a blessed hope, through Christ of entering thy glory."[2] Later that day he drove out of his gate, never to return. He had an appointment to preach at Bayswater the next day. His friend, Mr. Hobbs, drove him to his home in Bayswater where Clarke was to stay the night.

That evening several friends called. A Rev. Thomas Stanley tried to get Clarke to fix a time for a preaching date. Dr. Clarke replied, "I am not well; I cannot fix a time; I must first see what God is about to do with me."[3]

That night he became very ill. He was up and dressed, overcoat and all, at six on Sunday morning. He sent for his host, Mr. Hobbs. "My dear fellow," Clarke began, "you must get me home directly, without a miracle I could not preach; get me home—I want to be home."[4]

But before a carriage could be arranged, Adam was too sick to travel or even walk. Mrs. Hobbs and her daughter and a visiting lady sat him before a fire and rubbed his hands and forehead which had suddenly gone cold. Soon he was removed to a bedroom. Mr. Hobbs sent for several doctors, four in all. One was Adam's nephew, Thrascyles Clarke, a navy surgeon. All four of the doctors diagnosed cholera. Mr. Hobbs, upon this diagnosis, went to Clarke's bedside and said, "My dear doctor, you must put your soul into the hands of your God, and your trust in the merits of your Saviour." Adam replied faintly, "I do, I do."[5]

Clarke's sons, Theodoret and John Wesley Clarke, came to his bedside. His wife, Mary, arrived a little before four o'clock on that fateful Sunday afternoon. Adam feebly reached out his hand toward her when she entered. Adam's daughter, Mrs. Hook, was next to arrive, and the doctor weakly tried to clasp her hand. The last word that he spoke was to Theodoret when he briefly left the bedside about noon. "Are you going?" Clarke asked. Throughout the afternoon and the evening Clarke held on. The family and friends worked and waited. Mary refused to believe he was dying. She had seen him win so many health battles she thought he would do it again.

A few minutes after 11 p.m. Mr. Hobbs called Mary to the bedside, telling her that he was sure that the doctor was dying. Mary returned to the sickroom. "Surely, Mr. Hobbs, you are mistaken; Dr. Clarke breathes easier than he did just now."

"Yes, but shorter," Hobbs replied. At that moment Adam heaved a short sob, as physical life departed and his spirit returned to God. In his room they found written the text he had intended to preach on that day: "Verily, verily, I say unto you, The hour is coming, and now is, when the dead shall hear the voice of the Son of God: and they that hear shall live" (John 5:25).

Henry Moore, who knew Adam Clarke before he became a preacher and lived long enough to preach the funeral sermon, paid Clarke the highest tribute: "Our Connexion, I believe, never knew a more blameless life than that of Dr. Clarke. . . . He was, as Mr. Wesley used to say that a preacher . . . should be, without stain."[6]

Soon friends and converts joined the grieving family in the cemetery behind City Road Chapel. The Methodists gave Clarke the most honorable burial they could. They laid him in the same grave with the man he most admired in this life—John Wesley. As mourners ringed the open grave, they saw John Clarke step forward and drop something in the grave. It was a packet that contained a lock of hair from each of Adam's children and grandchildren. As the Clarkes slowly slipped away from the graveside, they did not even notice that the sun was shining. They would go home to discover on Adam's desk at the Heydon Hall house a poem he had written in a moment of meditative insight some weeks before:

### The Seasons of Adam Clarke's Life

I have enjoyed the *spring* of *life*—
I have endured the toils of its *summer*—
I have culled the fruits of its *autumn*,
I am now passing through the rigors of its *winter;*
And I am neither forsaken of *God*,
Nor abandoned by *man*.
I see at no great distance the dawn of a new day,
The first of a *spring* that shall be eternal.
   It is advancing to meet me!
   I run to embrace it!
Welcome! Welcome! eternal spring! Hallelujah![7]

Adam Clarke lies buried in London, but his legacy lives on. The focus of this chapter is on what Adam Clarke says to us today. He is more than an interesting footnote on the past. In a sense most of this book addresses this question. His choice of subjects, use of the Bible, powerful logic, skillful sermon structure, and preaching style all coach today's minister. In this chapter we shall celebrate Clarke's contribution to the Wesleyan legacy of biblical faith, sound doctrine, holy living, and loving our neighbor as ourselves.

## A Biblical Faith

The United States Government Printing Office publishes a 24-page booklet on how to detect counterfeit money. Test after test on how to check the validity of paper money is explained. After 23 pages it is further explained that a bill may pass all the tests so far discussed and still be counterfeit. Then the final test is described. The only way to tell for sure whether a bill is counterfeit or not, we are instructed, is to *compare it with one you know is good.*

For Adam Clarke all the winds of doctrine which howled through the winter of England's soul—deism, latitudinarianism, rationalism, dead orthodoxy—were to be examined and compared with the one certain, genuine, body of truth—the Bible. It was for Clarke the one Source in which we find "the truth, the whole truth and nothing but the truth."[8] In our day of "isms" galore which flourish like wisteria on the sunny side of the barn, examining them and all their claims in light of the Bible, like Wesley and Clarke would do, is a sound practice. Many scarlet scandals of selfishness and willfulness masquerading in the sheep's clothing of Christianity will have their wolfish hearts exposed.

We have already explored (in Chapter 3) Clarke's doctrine on the authority of the Bible, so there is no need to repeat it here. Suffice it to say that a biblical faith is not merely the sauce which seasons Wesleyanism; it is the meat, the main course, the substance of Wesleyanism itself.

## A HERITAGE OF SOUND DOCTRINE

From his journal we learn that when Adam Clarke served as president of the conference, he examined ministerial candidates on seven basic doctrines: original sin, the deity of Christ, the Atonement, justification by faith, Christian perfection, the witness of the Spirit, and eternal rewards and punishments. Add to this the doctrine of the Holy Scriptures already discussed, and you have a solid core of doctrine which accurately represents the teaching of the early Wesleyans. These doctrines pervaded the preaching of Adam Clarke (see Chapter 3) and should not be neglected by his theological descendants. This is not to say that Wesley, Clarke, Watson, etc. have had the final insight into Scripture, or that they have expressed every interpretation in a way that can never be improved. But it is to say that these doctrines are at the heart of Wesleyanism and are a part of the legacy of Adam Clarke.

### 1. *Original Sin*

Pelagianism rose out of its shallow grave during the 18th century and, robed in the words of John Taylor's *The Doctrine of Original Sin,* began to haunt the parishes and pulpits of England. Taylor's work, welcomed like Caspar the friendly ghost, declared that humans were born neutral and were either made holy and good or corrupt and evil by environment. John Wesley, as he said in a letter to Taylor, opposed it from "end to end."[9]

Wesley wrote one of his longest works, the *Doctrine of Original Sin* (1756), partially in response to Taylor's missile. In it he declared the essential orthodox doctrine of original sin. In his sermon "The Fall of Man" Wesley proclaimed that Adam "knowingly and deliberately rebelled against his Father. . . . In that moment he lost the moral image of God, and, in part, the natural: He commenced unholy, foolish, and unhappy. . . . He [Adam] entitled all his posterity to error, guilt, sorrow, fear, pain, diseases, and death."[10]

Adam Clarke and other Methodists taught this doctrine, with all its implications. Original sin and its results formed a major or minor theme of 28 of Clarke's 60 sermons. "Man is not what God made him,"[11] Clarke declared. Man was created in holiness, but a glance at society and history testify to the universal corruption of man. Clarke founded his doctrine on Genesis 3, Romans 5, and 1 Corinthians 15, as did Wesley. "The body, soul, and spirit of all the descendants of Adam must partake of his moral imperfections; for it is an . . . invariable law . . . that 'like shall produce its like.' We therefore," continues Clarke, "no longer hope to gather grapes off thorns or figs off thistles."[12] This sinful nature is demonstrated in a human race which "has a natural propensity to do evil."[13] The sin that ruined our first parents "has descended to all their posterity; and . . . incontestably proves that we are their legitimate offspring, the fallen progeny of fallen parents."[14]

Neither Wesley nor Clarke denied that environment had a great influence on people, but they said that was not sufficient to explain the scourge of sin. Clarke explained that all persons enter the world with the seeds of evil within. His environment will have much to say about how these seeds vegetate and express themselves. "All have the same seeds of evil; but not all have the same opportunity of cultivating these seeds."[15] But whether one's environment provides an opportunity for the flourishing of acquired depravity or whether it brings an atmosphere that represses sin, only the cleansing of sanctification can cure the disease of the nature out of joint with God.

Even though Clarke's statement of original sin is not expressed in popular psychological terms, most of us know what he was talking about when he wrote:

> There is a contagion in human nature, an evil principle, that is opposed to . . . God. This is the grand hidden cause of all transgression. It is a contagion from which no soul of man is free. . . . No human being was ever born without it. . . . It is commonly called original sin. . . . It is without conformity to the nature, will, and law of God; and is constantly in opposition to all three.[16]

The pivotal doctrine of original sin was challenged in the days of Wesley and Clarke. It is merely laughed off by the high priests of today, the behavioral scientists. The danger is that if the disease is denied and not discovered, the cure will not be sought or found.

## 2. *The Deity of Christ*

To Adam Clarke the deity of Christ was the most important point of Christology. On this point Clarke made an error of enthusiasm. In order to protect the deity of Christ, he challenged the doctrine of the eternal Sonship of Jesus. He felt that this gave to Christ a sort of second-place subjection that could lead to a denial of His deity. The next step, Clarke feared, was to make Him a created being. Perhaps we see here vestiges of the unitarian movement of the 17th century. Wesley admitted that he could not refute Clarke's claim, but wisely advised Clarke not to push this detail too hard lest division result. Clarke only partially complied.

Apart from that one point of difference, both Wesley and Clarke reaffirmed the traditional doctrines of the Nicene and Chalcedonian creeds on the deity of Christ. For them He was fully God and fully man. They preached Christ as Creator, Sustainer, Governor, and Redeemer.

Said Clarke, "The salvation of the whole human race stands or falls with the proper, essential, underived deity of Jesus Christ."[17] He also declared, "Take Deity away from any redeeming act of Christ, and redemption is ruined."[18] Take away the deity of Christ from Wesleyanism, and it too is ruined—a denatured caricature remains.

## 3. *Atonement*

The third doctrine about which Clarke quizzed the ministers-to-be was the doctrine of the Atonement. A candidate who espoused Abelard's moral influence theory or Calvin's limited atonement theory had no more chance of being ordained than if he had stood at that solemn hour before President Clarke quaffing gin and smoking a cigar.

Though John Wesley and Clarke as well had no thoroughgoing, detailed theory of atonement, their preaching and writing taught a substitutionary approach to understanding Christ's redeeming work. "He [Christ] put himself in the place of the whole human race," Clarke proclaimed, "for the very purpose of suffering in their stead. . . . Christ acted as a representative of, and substitute for, man: and thus not only made atonement for iniquity, but, by his merit, acquired a right for man to be restored to his forfeited privileges and to be brought back by adoption into the heavenly family."[19] Nothing short of Christ's atonement could save us. "Christ was man, that he might suffer and die for man; and he was God, that the sufferings and death of the man Christ Jesus might be of infinite value."[20]

The atonement of the Second Adam, who, representing all humankind, made himself an offering for sin, tasting death for everyone, is so effective that "no soul of man can ever be so deeply stained with sin from whose spirit God cannot extract that stain." Clarke went on to tell his audience in Hind Street Chapel, London, "All the transgressions you have committed against God may be pardoned, all the impurities of your souls may be extracted."[21]

## 4. *Justification by Faith*

To this day some people who ought to know better still think that Wesley and Wesleyans taught works-righteousness. True, Wesleyans have always believed in holy living, but they do not regard good works as coins to plunk down on the counter to pay for salvation. Nothing could be farther from the truth.

John Wesley said, "I believe justification is by faith alone, as much as I believe there is a God."[22] A year before his death Wesley wrote (1790), "About fifty years ago I had a clearer view than before of justification by faith; and in this . . . I have never varied, no, not a hair's breadth. Nevertheless, an ingenious man has publicly accused me of a thousand variations . . . but I still witness the same confession."[23]

Wesley saw justification as pardon or forgiveness of sins, acquittal from punishment for past sins, and acceptance or adoption into the family of God. Men and women are justified by "grace through faith, that faith is a personal trust, and the source of faith as well as grace is God."[24] Faith, for Wesley, was a sort of "grace made conscious in the individual"[25] and not faith in the sense of mental assent.

Justification by faith was a high-priority theme for Adam Clarke. It was a major or minor theme in 25 of the 60 sermons and was "honorably mentioned" in nearly all of them. One of his longest sermons was "Salvation by Faith." In that discourse he shows that justification cannot come through good works, suffering, penal suffering in purgatory, transmigration of souls, or from the mere benevolence of God. That the blood of Christ is the only avenue to justification, Clarke convincingly demonstrates. Like Wesley, Clarke was careful to let his hearers know that works-righteousness was a false hope. "Attachment to your creed . . . your discharge of religious and social duties may be good evidences of your sincerity," he said, "but they cannot atone for what is past, cleanse your fallen heart, or give you a title to . . . glory. . . . Jesus alone, and him crucified . . . takes away the sin of the world."[26] Though we hesitate to come before Him, for we have "a continual persuasion that we cannot be lovely in the sight of God, because we have done nothing but offend and grieve Him,"[27] we must come, knowing that it is the nature of "God's eternal mercy to do kindness to those who have no claims."[28]

In another document Clarke simply explains his doctrine:

> The doctrine of justification by faith is one of the grandest displays of the mercy of God to mankind. It is so very plain that all may comprehend it; and so free that all may attain it. What is more simple than this—Thou art a sinner, in consequence condemned to perdition, and utterly unable to save thy own soul. All are in the same state with thyself, and no man can give a ransom for the soul of his neighbour. God, in his mercy, has provided a Saviour for thee. As thy life was forfeited to death because of thy transgressions, Jesus Christ has redeemed thy life by giving up his own; he died in thy stead, and has made atonement to God for thy transgression; and offers thee the pardon he has thus purchased, on the simple condition that thou believe that his death is a sufficient sacrifice, ransom and oblation for thy sin; and that thou bring it, as such, by confident faith to the throne of God, and plead it in thy own behalf there. When thou dost so, thy faith shall be the means of receiving that salvation which Christ has bought by his blood.[29]

On justification by faith Clarke accurately reflected his mentor, Wesley. But at certain points (such as imputed righteousness) he was careful to put an additional "hair's breadth" between himself and the Calvinists.

## 5. *Christian Perfection*

A currently popular bumper sticker reads, "Christians Aren't Perfect—Just Forgiven." One wonders what President Clarke would have said had one of the young ordinands arrived at the conference with that sticker on his horse or carriage. As noted earlier, Clarke thought that the problem with Christians was stopping at forgiveness and not going on to perfection.

Clarke's preaching on holiness has already been explored in some detail in Chapter 9, so it need not be repeated here. Perhaps it should be pointed out, however, that Clarke had made some midcourse adjustments to Wesley's teachings. First, while Wesley strongly emphasized the processive *and* the crisis aspects of sanctification, Clarke, in the sermons, almost totally neglected the processive in favor of the crisis experience. He recognized a process and mentions it at least twice in his other writings, but in the pulpit the good news was that the Spirit can cleanse in the twinkling of an eye. One is tempted to believe, from the nomenclature of Clarke's preaching and writing, that Clarke had a fear that the *gradual* death to sin, allowed for at least in some of Wesley's teaching, results in *no* death to sin, or at least no *final* death to sin. He seems to urge longtime seekers to get on with it—find the crisis deliverance—or as some might want to say, complete the process, once and for all finding that *moment* when sin no longer lives within.

Another area of slight difference is Clarke's emphasis on Spirit language. If Clarke is read carefully, it is seen that he does preserve the Christocentric nature of Wesleyanism. But the casual hearer or reader might—repeat, *might*—come away more aware of the pneumatological concerns.

In these two points one is tempted to see in Clarke a stepping-stone between earliest Methodism and the earliest (before 1885) American Holiness Movement. Clarke is not a *bridge* between them, but possibly a stepping-stone.

But all of this aside, the part of the Clarke legacy on holiness which should stir us most may be the reminder he gives us of the urgency of the matter. Timing is so important in human affairs. After reading Clarke, you feel like the tide of time again is presenting us a crest of opportunity to preach and teach this doctrine with new vitality and relevance.

Are those forces which seemed to conspire against scriptural holiness in the days of Wesley and Clarke still afoot? It may be that the forces which make holiness of heart and life seem impossible and thus unsought have diversified and expanded, and are more subtle than ever. They are not only afoot but quietly dominate the scene.

One such force is behavioristic or deterministic psychology. Those of the ilk of B. F. Skinner say that autonomous man is dead, and good riddance; he never existed anyway. Now we know that man is just conscious automata, a lump upon which the environment acts. We have noted that this is a sort of secular Bezan Calvinism with no vertical dimension. And if we could truly see how this thought pattern saturates the *assumptions* of our society, we would be alarmed.

Another such force is the new humanism, typified by the human potential movement. It has become a kind of secular Pelagianism with no vertical dimension. It spreads like poison ivy the idea that man is not sinful anyway. What an archaic notion—sin. Don't try to save people; there is really no sin to save them from.

Adam Clarke had to overcome a world drenched in

174

the ideas that sanctification came by penal suffering (purgatory) or in the hour and article of death. Today, even more disturbing views are advanced by determinists and the new humanism. To the determinists, holiness is a mere amusing pun on human nature that is completely beside the point. To the new humanism, holiness is a pitiable, not-quite-funny non sequitur.

Perhaps the challenge and need for preaching holiness, God's will *in* us, has never been greater. Holiness—has not her time returned? What do men and women need more to hear than that by God's grace, Christ's atonement, and the indwelling, purifying presence of Christ's Holy Spirit, the springs of the soul can flow crystal clear, clean, and pure.

## 6. *The Witness of the Spirit*

The Wesleyan doctrine of the direct witness of the Spirit to the believer was more than the theologians of England could gag down. Wesley and his followers were berated as fanatics. Bishop Butler is reported to have charged Wesley to his face, "Sir, the pretending to extraordinary revelations and gifts of the Holy Ghost is a very horrid thing, a very horrid thing."[30] But to men like Wesley and Clarke, Scripture, reason, and experience all testified to the truth of assurance. Wesley spoke of his Aldersgate experience in validating the biblical doctrine of assurance, and Clarke spoke of his experience in the field where he first sensed God's Spirit bearing witness with his spirit that he was a child of God. Fifty-two years later, in a rare personal illustration, he told of that experience. "The report got spread that 'little Adam Clarke' had obtained the faith of assurance. Yes, glory be to God! I had got it—and what is more I still have it."[31]

John Wesley described the witness of the Spirit as "an inward impression on the soul, whereby the Spirit of God

175

directly witnesses to my spirit, that I am a child of God; that Jesus hath loved me, and given himself for me; and that all my sins are blotted out, and I, even I, am reconciled to God."[32] Clarke echoed similar statements again and again, thus handing on to the next century a truly Wesleyan doctrine of assurance.

It is such an important matter "to every Christian soul," Clarke affirmed, "that God in His mercy has been pleased not to leave it to conjecture, assumption, or inductive reasoning; but attests it by his own Spirit in the soul."[33] Here is part of what he said on this subject in the sermon "Experimental Religion and Its Fruits":

1. Spiritual sense produces what is called experimental religion—the life of God in the soul of man. This mental perception, or heart-feeling, answers in religion to palpable experience in philosophy. A simple conviction, and knowledge of bodies and their properties, is widely different from this spiritual feeling. By the sense of feeling we gain a knowledge or perception of bodies and their qualities; of hard, soft, wet, dry, cold, hot, and other tangible properties; yet this gives us no mental feeling of those qualities, so as to demonstrate their truth. But that which is mentioned by the apostle implies this feeling, this mental, internal sense and in this consists the great difference between theoretical and experimental religion.

2. The apostle, in another place, explains this spiritual sense in one word: "And because ye are sons, God hath sent forth the Spirit of his Son into your hearts, crying Abba, Father. For the Spirit himself beareth witness with our spirits, that we are the children of God." Now the fact to be witnessed is beyond the knowledge of man; no human power or cunning can acquire it; if obtained at all, it must come from above. In this human wit and ingenuity can do nothing. The Spirit himself comes to tell us that we are reconciled to God—that our sins are blotted out—that we are adopted into the family of heaven. The apostle tells us that this is witnessed by the Spirit of God. God

alone can tell whom he has accepted—whose sins he has blotted out—whom he has put among his children; this he makes known by his Spirit, in our spirit; so that we have, not by induction or inference, a thorough conviction and mental feeling that we are his children.

3. There is as great a difference between this and knowledge gained by logical argument.[34]

Besides finding numerous scriptures which "most positively assert it," the doctrine of "experimental" religion made a lot of sense to Adam Clarke. He found it strange that a person could be born again, have all the guilt of all the sins of all the past removed, have the Adamic nature cleansed from all sin, have all unholy tempers removed, and have his heart and life filled with the presence and fruit of the Holy Spirit—and not know about it.

In one of his sermons, "God's Love in Christ," he exhorted:

Believe an old man who has studied this matter longer, perhaps, than any or most of you have lived. Believe him, after having tried by every rule of reason of which he is master, he is obliged to come to this—that there can be no genuine happiness on this side of heaven, nor assurance . . . unless God has a testimony to give to the conscience . . . that he . . . is born of God, and is a child of the Most High.[35]

## 7. *Eternal Rewards and Punishments*

The seventh point of doctrine on which Clarke examined the ministerial candidates had to do with heaven and hell.

a. *Hell.* Hell was a major theme in only 1 of Clarke's 60 published sermons. It was a minor theme in 7 others. And apparently he considered it a doctrine which young preachers in the making needed to understand.

In Clarke's preaching he admitted that there were some things about hell that he did not understand. Fur-

177

ther, some of the imaginative descriptions of it were not to be trusted. There were some things, however, which he said we could know about it.

(1) All the finally impenitent would go there.

(2) It is eternal in duration. "When we can prove that the gospel shall be preached in hell, and offers of salvation, free, full, and present, be made to the damned, then we may expect that the worm that dieth not, shall die; and the fire that is not quenched, shall burn out!"[36]

(3) The eternal destruction of hell is not annihilation.

(4) Nor is it a purgatorial term that will come to an end.

(5) Torments there include regret, remorse, a view of the blessed, and final separation from God.

(6) The best thing of all about hell is that in God's unlimited grace no one has to go there, for "God does not show us a perdition that cannot be avoided, nor a heaven we cannot attain."[37] "Hell was made for only the devil and his angels, not for man;—man is an intruder into it; no human spirit shall ever be found there but through its own fault."[38]

b. *Heaven.* Clarke preached on heaven a little more than on hell. The eternal abode of the redeemed was a major theme in one of the sermons and a minor theme in nine others.

Clarke affirms 10 things about heaven.

(1) Heaven is for the holy angels and the spirits of just men made perfect, for all those "heirs of God" who have believed unto salvation.

(2) In heaven there will be no sin, suffering, pain, or evil.

(3) Complete satisfaction for all the desires of the soul shall be available.

(4) The body shall be fashioned after Christ's.

(5) The redeemed will reign with God.

(6) The "heirs" of God shall inherit God himself—He will be their portion. How wonderful is the lot of the redeemed. "A child of corruption, lately a slave of sin and heir of perdition; tossed about with every storm of life; in afflictions many and privations oft; having perhaps scarcely where to lay his head; and at last prostrated by death, and mingled with the dust of the earth; but now how changed!"[39]

(7) The joys and duration of heaven are timeless.

(8) Any soul, no matter how wretched, can be saved, sanctified, and fitted for heaven.

(9) Heaven is a "region" where *growth* and *service* thrive and expand.

(10) "It is vain to attempt to describe this state."[40]

These seven doctrines do not exhaust Clarke's theology. It is beyond the scope of this book to try to systematize all of Clarke's theological writings (this has already been done with modest success by Samuel Dunn). Nevertheless, we see in these doctrines the theological legacy Clarke bequeathed to the current generation of Wesleyans. Which of these doctrines dare we not give regular attention to in our teaching, preaching, and writing?

## THE HALLMARK OF HOLINESS

Some American groups need to get in touch with their early English Wesleyan roots, especially on the matter of the evidence of the sanctified life. Clarke (as well as Wesley) reminds us that the hallmark of holiness is *love*. As Clarke said again and again, the goal of the sanctified is to "perfectly love God and their neighbors as themselves."

The Wesleyans lived disciplined lives—but the hallmark of the holy life was *love*.

Adam Clarke spoke against cheap novels, charging

more than 5 percent interest, and church choirs—but the hallmark of the holy life was *love*.

Clarke opposed tea, gambling, and dancing—but the hallmark of the holy life was *love*.

Clarke insisted on fermented wine for Communion, but he registered negative opinions about tobacco, Sabbath breaking, drunkenness, and musical instruments in the church—but the hallmark of the holy life was *love*.

When Wesleyanism was shipped across the Atlantic, somebody turned the package upside down; and some of those who received the shipment thought that the hallmark of holiness was the keeping of a long list of rules to the neglect of perfect love. Being myth-makers by nature, it is so easy for us to examine the lives of our heroes and make their opinions and peculiar habits our laws for living. These are so much easier to identify and easier to live by than the law of perfect love. This is not to say that disciplined conduct is not important. The early Wesleyans believed in and practiced strict personal piety. It is vital to Christian living now, even though today it is about as popular as chapped lips. However, if we substitute a code of conduct for "perfectly loving God and loving our neighbor as ourselves," we have made the mistake of Rehoboam. He was the one, you remember, who took down the shields of gold from God's Temple and replaced them with shields of brass (1 Kings 14:26-27).

From Clarke's sermons one would have a difficult time forging shields of brass. The good news of the golden shields of perfect love glisten throughout. But from his journal and letters we find his sometimes stubborn opinions and his personal disciplines. If we pick the private or peculiar preferences, opinions, or patterns of behavior of Clarke or Wesley or Daniel Steele or any other holiness hero and concoct from them an ironbound code of conduct, we nullify the heart of the tradition and shift the focus from *love* to rule keeping.

You see, I could avoid tea, tobacco, and dancing; eschew piano lessons; put cotton in my ears when the choir sings; keep 39 other rules; and still I might not have a heart ruled by love.

Clarke preached that in sanctification the Holy Spirit would purge away all "unholy tempers" (pride, deceit, hatred, bitterness, etc.). In their place the fruit of the Spirit would grow. "To be filled with all the fullness of God is to have the heart emptied of and cleansed from all sin and defilement," Clarke said, "and filled with humility, meekness, gentleness, goodness, justice, holiness, mercy, and truth and love to God and man."[41] In the same sermon he adds that sanctification will produce loving obedience to God and "unvarying benevolence toward one's neighbor."[42]

The "fullness of the Gospel of Jesus" will bring about "a holy frame of soul, a holy heart full of pure and righteous tempers, affections and desires"[43] and "a heart reconciled to and wholly influenced and governed by the spirit of . . . benevolence which dwelt in the Lord Jesus."[44] In this way alone will the Christian be able "perfectly to love God and worthily magnify his holy name."[45]

Clarke, as Christ's ambassador, teaches us today that love is the hallmark of the holy life. The holy life of love is carried out by sincere devotion, loving obedience, much private prayer, worship with others, and vigorous service to our neighbor. The witness of the Spirit is to be accompanied by the confirming witness of the fruit of the Spirit in both heart and life. To a friend who was seeking to live such a Christian life, Clarke gave this advice:

> Pray much in private. Without this you will find it utterly impossible to keep yourself in the love of God. No soul that prays much in private ever falls. Apos-

tasy from God can never begin until private prayer is carelessly used or abandoned. Read the blessed book of God. Let his testimonies be your counselors and let the matter of them be your song in the night. Keep closely united to God's people. Do not omit one class meeting even in a year if you can possibly avoid it. I have been now a traveling preacher upward of 24 years and yet I feel class meeting as necessary now as I did when I began. You may think it strange to hear that I meet regularly once a week and have done so for years. I find it great privilege to forget that I am a preacher and come with simple heart to receive instruction from my leader. Look for full salvation, have every temper and desire brought under the will of God. Do not live without the witness of the Spirit. Carry Christ about with you and recommend Him to all.[46]

## WE ARE SERVANTS OF CHRIST'S LOVE

The Christian not only seeks to "perfectly love God" but to love his human brothers everywhere. This love concerns itself with both the spiritual and temporal well-being of others. Clarke taught his eager listeners that "our Lord shows us that acts of kindness are to be done to any person in distress, of whatever nation, religion, or kindred."[47] He further stated in the same sermon, "We should rejoice in his [our neighbor's] happiness, mourn his adversity . . . delight in his prosperity, and promote it to the best of our power; instruct his ignorance, help his weakness, and risk even our life for his sake."[48]

Clarke's own creed of servant living and loving others is recorded in a letter to his friend, James Everett.

God never needed my services: He brought me into the world that I might receive good from him, and do good to my fellows. This is God's object in reference to all human beings, and should be the object of every man in reference to his brother. This is the whole of my practical creed. God, in his love, gave me a being: in his mercy he has done everything he should do, to make it a well-being; has taught me to love him, by first loving me; and has taught me to love my neighbour as myself, by inspiring me with his own love. Therefore, my grand object, in all my best and considerate moments, is, to live to get good from God, that I may do good to my fellows; and this alone is the way in which man can glorify his Maker.[49]

The social context which Wesley, Clarke, and the early Methodists confronted is strangely like our own. It was a day of overwhelming social problems. There were no easy answers—in fact, it seemed there were no answers at all.

The primary arena of the social problems, like today, was the cities. England was moving from a rural, agrarian society to an urban, industrial society. The Industrial Revolution blew humanity into the cities of London, Manchester, and Liverpool like maple leaves before a fierce autumn wind. And it left them, like leaves, piled up in random heaps. Housing conditions were outrageous. Ten persons per unfurnished room was common. They slept on sawdust or wood shavings on the floor. Horse manure polluted the unpaved streets. In London it was sometimes piled 14 feet high on both sides of the street.

Diseases like typhoid, smallpox, dysentery, and cholera raged and ravaged like monsters in a nightmare. One-fourth of the babies born died the first week of their lives. Every day the whirlwind of industrialization blew in more people, and every day more died from exposure, disease, crime, and malnutrition. In many cities the graveyard operators maintained "poor holes"—large, common graves left open until they were filled up. Is it any wonder that John Wesley wrote a book on basic health? Or that Adam Clarke took time out from pastoral duties to go to medical school for a year?

Crimes of rape, murder, robbery, rioting, and looting were as common as dandelions in the backyard. Gambling on every imaginable thing became the national pastime.[50] Gin became the opiate of the people, the temporary savior to which the masses turned for momentary solace.

While most people could not muster the courage to even contemplate these massive problems, the Methodists resolutely confronted them in the name of Jesus. They came up with relief for the poor, schools for the illiterate, hospitals for the sick, clothes for the naked, and salvation and hope for the soul. More than anything else, perhaps, Wesley, Clarke, and the Methodists helped these sorrowful victims of squalor see their essential dignity before God. To a crowded out April, 1820, congregation in City Road Chapel, London, Adam Clarke cried out, "Show me . . . the vilest wretch in . . . London, and I say, that he has the same claim upon God's mercy as the apostles had, and may have as much mercy as they had . . . to qualify them for the kingdom of heaven."[51] What do the millions of people who populate the ghettos of North America, the refugee camps of Asia, the famine belt in Africa need to hear from the modern Wesleyans? They need food, clothing, medicine, and love. And they, too, need to see their essential dignity before God and a Redeemer who gave himself for them.

Clarke and Company have modeled for us a near perfect marriage of personal religion and social responsibility. It may be that some of us who take the name Wesleyan have most nearly betrayed our heritage at this point. Some of us have ignored the crushing problems of the people for whom Christ died, choosing rather to retreat into our conventicles of worship to sing sweet songs about the trees, sky, and flowers. On the other hand, some of us have all but forsaken the Wesleyan experience of life-changing personal religion and inward holiness, yet vigorously pursue social change, acting out a new brand of salvation by works. The true Wesleyan is both *holy* and *helpful*.

Perhaps the time for the renewal of Wesleyanism has come again. Like the early Wesleyan era, we face seemingly insurmountable social problems. They had overcrowded cities; we have even more of that commodity. They faced poverty, illiteracy, and diease; we face such things as well. They tried to feed the hungry; our earth is haunted by hunger. They dealt with gin and tobacco; our drug problems are even more sophisticated. They shouted down slavery in their world; our global village is pockmarked with human oppression, too.

May God send us more Wesleys and more Clarkes who will declare as Adam Clarke did, "I must go on till he [God] stops me. To sacrifice my life at the command, or in the work of God is, as to pain or difficulty, no more to me than a burnt straw: my life is his."[52] At the age of 72, just three months before his exhausted body gave up the ghost, Clarke wrote to Mary, his wife, "I shall pocket and seal up all my causes of complaint; join myself to the forlorn hope, at the front of the storming party, and mount the breach for the God of armies in the defence of his people!"[53]

In light of the rich legacy Adam Clarke has willed us, worse things could happen than to have the vitality of Adam Clarke return to be a stirring spirit among us. Would anyone like to sing along with this poem?

### I'D GLADLY LET THIS MAN LEAD ME

*The commentator, Adam Clarke,*
*Helped Methodism to embark*
*By publishing the Bible's sense*
*In careful, thoughtful eloquence.*

*From then till now we've hardly known*
*If meanings given were our own;*

We'd so imbibed what Clarke had said,
It might have come from that man's head.

But this real early troubadour
Did for the movement much, much more,
As pastor for some fifty years—
A good one, too, it quite appears.

The fifteen thousand times he preached
Was one important way he reached
The people of his wayward day
Who by their sins had gone astray.

He preached on second blessing themes,
On how the Holy God redeems
From sin in state as well as act,
According to a gracious pact.

He visited the sick, the poor,
And left a pastor's signature
On thousands in his church and town
Who never saw an Oxford gown.

And when he'd meet a man in need,
The need would with his heart so plead,
He'd give the man his coat to use,
Or he'd go home without his shoes.

Three times he led the Methodists;
And something in my heart insists,
Because I'm such a devotee,
I'd gladly let this man lead me.[54]

—J. KENNETH GRIDER

# 13

# The Quotable Adam Clarke

Hundreds of quotations from Clarke have already been cited in this book. Nevertheless, more selected quotations from Clarke's sermons and other writings are presented here.

## Attitude

"It is astonishing that any who profess the Christian name should indulge bitterness of spirit. Those who are censorious, who are unmerciful to the failings of others, who have fixed a certain standard by which they measure all persons in all circumstances, and unchristianize every one that does not come up to this standard, they have the bitterness against which the apostle speaks. In the last century there was a compound medicine, made up from a variety of drastic acid drugs and ardent spirits, which was called, *hiera piera,* the *holy bitter;* this medicine was administered in a multitude of cases, where it did immense evil, and perhaps in scarcely any case did it do good. It has ever appeared to furnish a proper epithet for the disposition mentioned above, the *holy bitter,* for the religiously censorious act under the pretence of superior sanctity. I have known such persons do much evil in a Christian society, but never knew an instance of their doing any good."

*Theology,* p. 175

### Character
"The thoroughly honest man needs no oath to bind him—his character swears for him; we have need only of a little reflection to convince us, that he who will not be honest without an oath, will not be honest with one."

*Sermons,* 2:113

### Christ
"Suppose Christ attended by all the hosts of heaven, and about to create a *new* system—all the sons of God anxiously waiting the omnific word, which was to call the whole into being, order, and beauty,—a voice from earth should reach his ear,—'Jesus, thou son of David, have mercy on me;' I tell you, brethren, if it were necessary for him to *leave undone* one thing to *do another,* he would leave worlds uncreated, to answer the cry of a poor perishing sinner."

Everett, 1:220

"Hear him [Jesus] *preaching*—see him suffering, dying, rising, reigning; and you can never more be troubled with doubts concerning the goodness of God, and his readiness to save to the uttermost."

*Sermons,* 1:366

"If Christianity be not true, there is no religion on earth, for no other religion is worth a rush to man's salvation; if we have not redemption in Jesus, there is no other Saviour. If not justified through his blood, and sanctified by his Spirit, there is no final happiness. . . . But there is a Christ, there is redemption through his blood; I have this redemption, and I am waiting for the fulness of the blessing of the Gospel of Jesus."

J. B. B. Clarke, 3:206

"The hope of pardon, holiness, and heaven, depends wholly on the resurrection of Jesus."

*Sermons,* 1:354

"Other refuge for the miserable—other name as the object of faith—other sacrifice as an atonement for sin— other help or saviour is not found."

*Sermons,* 2:253

### The Church
"May its friends never corrupt it [the church]; for, as to its enemies, they can never prevail against it."

*Sermons,* 2:231

"There is no danger so imminent, both to yourselves and to us, as departing from our original simplicity in spirit, in manners, and in our mode of worship. As the world is continually changing around us, we are liable to be affected by those changes. We think, in many cases, that we may please well-intentioned men better, and be more useful to them, by permitting many of the more innocent forms of the world to enter into the *church;* wherever we have done so, we have infallibly lost ground in the depth of our religion, and in its spirituality and unction. I would say to all, keep your doctrines and your discipline, not only in your church-books and society-rules, but preach the former without refining upon them—observe the latter without bending it to circumstances, or impairing its vigour by frivolous exceptions and partialities."

Letter to American Methodists, Everett, 2:272

## Conversion

"No man should consider his repentance as having answered a saving end to his soul, till he feels that God for Christ's sake has forgiven him his sins; and the Spirit of God testifies with his spirit that he is a child of God . . . [to] cause the people to rest short of this, to be satisfied with . . . problematic repentance and conversion, [is] . . . crying, 'Peace! Peace!' where God has not spoken peace."

*Sermons,* 2:255

"So deep is the stain, so radicated the habits of sinning, so strong the propensity to do what is evil; that nothing less than the power by which the soul was created, can conquer these habits, eradicate these vices, and cause such a leper to change his spots, and such an Ethiop his hue. The whole change which the soul undergoes in its conversion, is the effect of a divine energy within."

*Theology,* p. 147

## Credit

"Be prudent; be cautious; neither eat, drink, nor wear, but as you pay for every thing. Live not on trust, for that is the way to pay double; and by this means the poor are still kept poor. He who takes credit, even for food or raiment, when he has no probable means of defraying the debt, is a dishonest man."

*Theology,* p. 291

## Discipleship

"To him who loves God with all his heart, the fulfillment of duty is not only possible, but easy and delightful."

*Sermons,* 2:173

"By the finger of God the moral law is written on his

heart, and by incessant acts of loving obedience it is transcribed in his life."

*Sermons,* 1:209

"He has respect to all God's commandments;—should each have a cross in it, he takes up that cross."

*Sermons,* 2:100

"Carefulness, circumspection, and diligence are never prohibited by the gospel."

*Sermons,* 1:378

"In subjection and obedience all good is secured; in disaffection and rebellion, all good is forfeited."

*Sermons,* 1:387

"He who lives not in the due performance of every Christian duty, whatever faith he may profess, is either a vile hypocrite or a scandalous Antinomian."

*Theology,* p. 140

"How can we be said to credit conscientiously the doctrines of Christianity, and live satisfied with such slender attainments in the divine life."

*Sermons,* 1:307

### Eternal Rewards and Punishments

"There is no injustice in hell, more than there is in heaven. He who does not deserve it, shall never fall into the bitter pains of an eternal death; and no man shall ever eat of the tree of life in heaven who has not a right to it."

*Sermons,* 2:78

"Every sinner earns everlasting perdition by long, sore, and painful service. O what pains do men take to get to hell! Early and late they toil at sin; and would not divine justice be in their debt, if it did not pay them their due wages?"

*Theology,* p. 372

"Sinners may lose their time in disputing against the reality of hell fire, till awakened to a sense of their folly, by finding themselves plunged into what God calls 'the lake that burns with fire and brimstone.' . . . the punishment [the words] point out is awful, horrible, and real, beyond the power of language to describe, or thought to reach."

*Sermons,* 4:25

"We think it a grand thing not to go to hell; but if I cannot go to heaven, it seems to me a matter of little consequence if I go to hell."

*Sermons,* 4:180

### Evil Speaking

"Drive them [evil speakers] from thy door, yet labour to convert them if thou canst; but if they continue as disturbers . . . of the union of Christ's church, let them be to thee . . . the basest, the lowermost, the most dejected, most underfoot, and down-trodden vassals of perdition."

*Sermons,* 2:110

"The backbiter [is] the man with the three-forked tongue: with it he wounds three persons at the same time —the man whom he slanders, the man who receives the slander, and himself . . . the slanderer."

*Sermons,* 2:105

"The person . . . may have been tempted and overcome—may have been wounded in the cloudy and dark day; and now deeply mourns his fall before God. Who, that has not the heart of a demon, would not strive rather to cover, than to make bare the fault."

*Sermons,* 2:107

### Faith

"It is as much thy duty to strive to *believe,* as it is to strive to *pray.*"

*Sermons,* 2:385

"God requires, yea commands, men to believe, and threatens them with perdition if they do not; for he no more believes for men, than he repents, loves, or obeys for them."

*Sermons,* 1:207

### False Teachers

"The doctrine and teacher most prized and followed by worldly men, and by the gay, giddy, and garish multitude, are not from God; they savour of the flesh, lay on no restraints, prescribe no cross-bearing, and leave every one in full possession of his heart's lusts and easily besetting sins. And by this, false doctrine and false teachers are easily discerned."

*Theology,* p. 333

### Family

"It is easier for most men to walk with a perfect heart in the church, or even the world, than their own families. How many are as meek as lambs among others, when at home they are wasps or tigers!"

*Theology,* p. 275

"He who corrects his children according to God and reason will feel every blow on his own heart more sensibly than his child feels it on his body. Parents are called to correct, not to punish, their children."

*Theology,* p. 274

"Parental affection, when alone, infallibly degenerates into foolish fondness; and parental authority frequently degenerates into brutal tyranny when standing by itself. The first sort of parents will be loved, without being respected; the second sort will be dreaded, without either respect or esteem."

*Theology,* p. 273

"Early habits are not easily rooted out, especially those of a bad kind. Next to the influence and grace of the Spirit of God is a good and religious education. Parents should teach their children to despise and abhor low cunning, to fear a lie, and tremble at an oath; and, in order to be successful, they should illustrate their precepts by their own regular and conscientious example."

*Theology,* p. 272

"A most injurious and destructive maxim has lately been advanced by a few individuals, which it is to be hoped is disowned by the class of Christians to which they belong, though the authors affect to be thought Christians, and rational ones too. The sum of the maxim is this: 'Children ought not to be taught religion, for fear of having their minds biased to some particular creed; but they should be left to themselves till they are capable of making a choice, and choose to make one.'"

*Theology,* p. 269

"The husband is to love his wife, the wife to obey and venerate her husband; love and protection on the one hand, affectionate submission and fidelity on the other. The husband should provide for his wife without encouraging profuseness; watch over her conduct without giving her vexation; keep her in subjection without making her a slave; love her without jealousy; oblige her without flattery; honour her without making her proud; and be hers entirely, without becoming either her footman or her slave. In short, they have equal rights and equal claims; but superior strength gives the man dominion; affection and subjection entitle the woman to love and protection. Without the woman, man is but half a human being; in union with the man, the woman finds her safety and perfection."

*Theology,* p. 263

"'A man shall leave,' wholly give up, 'both father and mother'; the matrimonial union being more intimate and binding than even paternal or filial affection: and shall be closely united; shall be firmly cemented to his wife: a beautiful metaphor, which most forcibly intimates that nothing but death can separate them: as a well glued board will break sooner in the whole wood than in the glued joint."

*Theology,* p. 262

## God/Providence

"You [Christians] can call God Father, as legitimately as you can call him God."

*Sermons,* 4:378

"The system of humanizing God, and making him, by our unjust conceptions of him, to act as ourselves would in certain circumstances, has been the bane both of religion and piety; and on this ground infidels have laughed us to scorn."

*Theology,* p. 75

"Those who can approach him [God] without terror know little of his justice, and nothing of their sins."

*Theology,* p. 80

"God never punishes any but those who deserve it; but he blesses incessantly those who deserve it not. The reason is evident: justice depends on certain rules; but beneficence is free."

*Theology,* p. 76

"The whole human race are objects of the love of God. Every . . . drunkard . . . every sabbath-breaker . . . every lover of money . . . every devil-like . . . soul among you is an object of the infinite love . . . of God."

*Sermons,* 4:174

"They who acquaint themselves with God, will find him to be their friend, their highest, chiefest, and best friend—a friend that loveth at all times—that knows the souls of his followers in adversity."

*Sermons,* 2:138

"Men . . . by making an improper use of God's mercies, strip themselves, as it were of God's blessings, and keep themselves in . . . unnecessary poverty."

*Sermons,* 4:201

"He [God] is too wise to err, and too good to do anything that is unkind. He loves you, and will cause every thing to work for your own good."

J. B. B. Clarke, Letter to a friend
who had just lost his wife, 2:43

"He [God] is continually among you; his eye is upon you; there is no want of yours, no necessity of yours, he does not see; there is nothing he undertakes that he does not accomplish."

*Sermons,* 4:88

### Grace

"While *sinners,* we are in debt to infinite justice; when pardoned, in debt to endless *mercy.*"

*Sermons,* 2:27

"Nothing can produce this salvation but the power of God, so no one can merit it; none can purchase it by works . . . therefore it is a gratuitous offer made to mankind."

*Sermons,* 6:155

## Gratitude

"He loves man, wheresoever found, of whatsoever colour, in whatever circumstances, and in all stages of his pilgrimage from his cradle to his grave. Let the lisp of the infant, the shout of the adult, and the sigh of the aged, ascend to the universal Parent, as a gratitude-offering."

*Theology,* p. 242

"When the mouth is full of meat, it is natural to look for a thankful heart."

*Sermons,* 3:296

## Happiness

"A man may have as many houses as he can inhabit, as many clothes as he can wear, as many beds as he can lie on, and as much food as he can eat and, with all, possess sound health and strength; and yet his soul be in misery."

*Theology,* p. 390

"He who gives his heart to the world robs God of it; and, in snatching at the shadow of earthly good, loses substantial and eternal blessedness."

*Theology,* p. 289

"The whole human race are wrong, . . . all are running themselves out of breath for no prize. They are seeking, not that which can make an immortal spirit happy, but that which can gratify and content the animal nature."

*Sermons,* 1:348

"Happiness . . . consisted in having the animal nature subjected to the rational. In order to do this [find happiness], they took incredible pains, invented copious rules, and prescribed ascetic discipline . . . But alas, all was in vain; the *animal* rose above the *rational;* and the *brute* ran away with the *man.*"

*Sermons,* 1:242

## Holiness

"Cleansed people never forget the horrible pit and miry clay out of which they have been brought. And can they then be proud? No! They loathe themselves in their own sight. They can never forgive themselves for having sinned against so good a God and so loving a Saviour. And can they undervalue him by whose blood they were bought, and by whose blood they were cleansed? No!"

*Theology,* p. 209

"Let all those who retain the apostolic doctrine, that the blood of Christ cleanseth from all sin in this life, press every believer to go on to perfection."

*Theology,* p. 201

"Would not the grace and power of Christ appear more conspicuous in slaying the lion than in keeping him chained? in destroying sin, root and branch, and filling the soul with his own holiness, with love to God and man, with the mind, all the holy, heavenly tempers that were in himself, than in leaving these impure and unholy tempers ever to live, and often to reign, in the heart?"

*Theology,* p. 201

"Every man whose heart is full of the love of God is full of humility; for there is no man so humble as he whose heart is cleansed from all sin. It has been said that indwelling sin humbles us; never was there a greater falsity: pride is the very essence of sin; he who has sin has pride; and pride, too, in proportion to his sin."

*Theology,* pp. 205-6

"It [the gospel] does not act by laying on restraints, but by eradicating evils; it not only takes away those evil dispositions which lead to the works of the devil and the flesh, but it infuses those principles which lead to peace, purity, and happiness."

*Sermons,* 1:151

"God is holy; and this is the eternal reason why all his people should be holy—should be purified from all filthiness of the flesh and spirit, perfecting holiness in the fear of God."

*Theology,* p. 199

"The whole design of God was to restore man to his image, and raise him from the ruins of his fall; in a word, to make him perfect; to blot out all his sins, purify his soul, and fill him with holiness; so that no unholy temper, evil desire, or impure affection or passion shall either lodge, or have any being within him; this and this only is true religion, or Christian perfection; and a less salvation than this would be dishonourable to the sacrifice of Christ, and the operation of the Holy Ghost; and would be as unworthy of the appellation of 'Christianity,' as it would be of that 'holiness or perfection.'"

*Theology,* p. 200

"Sanctification or holiness . . . is progressive, as a growing up into Jesus Christ, our living Head, in all things; and may be instantaneous, as God can, and often does, empty the soul of all sin in a moment, in the twinkling of an eye; and then, having sowed in the seeds of righteousness, they have a free and unmolested vegetation."

*Theology,* p. 148

"If men would but spend as much time fervently calling upon God to cleanse . . . as they spend in decrying this doctrine, what a glorious state of the church should we soon witness."

*Sermons,* 3:289

"Had I no other proof that man is wholly fallen from God, his opposition to Christian holiness would be too sufficient."

*Sermons,* 3:279

"Let none expect that God will purify his heart, while he is knowingly indulging any of its evil propensities."

*Sermons,* 1:301

## Holy Spirit

"The Holy Spirit in the soul of a believer is God's seal, set on his heart to testify that he is God's property, and that he should be wholly employed in God's service.

"As Christ is represented as the ambassador of the Father, so the Holy Spirit is represented as the ambassador of the Son, coming vested with his authority, as the interpreter and executor of his will."

*Theology,* p. 157

"To purify the soul, to refine and sublime all the passions and appetites, the operation of the Holy Spirit is promised. Spirit only can act successfully on spirit; and this Spirit is called the Holy Spirit, not only because it is holy in itself, but because it is the Author of holiness to them who receive it."

*Theology,* pp. 160-61

"God promised his Holy Spirit to sanctify and cleanse the heart, so as utterly to destroy all pride, anger, self-will, peevishness, hatred, malice, and every thing contrary to his own holiness.

"The very Spirit which is given them, on their believing in Christ Jesus, is the Spirit of holiness; and they can retain this Spirit no longer than they live in the spirit of obedience."

*Theology,* p. 162

"The work of the Spirit is to refine and rectify the passions of man; not to create new ones, nor to destroy old ones, but to influence, purify, regulate, direct, and moderate the whole. We did not lose one passion by the FALL; we do not gain one by regeneration."

*Sermons,* 1:372

## Hope

"Fruitless longings drink up the spirit . . . Hope . . . utterly disappointed, slays it."

*Sermons,* 1:372

## Human Nature

"Fickleness is the character of man next to sinfulness. He is never at one stay; if he is constant to anything . . . it is to his unsteadiness to his own purposes."

*Sermons,* 4:111

"Nothing in the history of society is so inexplicable as the proneness to believe in quackery."

*Sermons,* 2:80

## Learning

"A truly learned man is ever humble and complacent; and one who is under the influence of the divine Spirit is ever meek, gentle, and easy to be entreated. The proud and the insolent are neither Christians nor scholars. Both religion and learning disclaim them, as being a disgrace to both."

*Theology,* p. 299

"Sound learning is of great worth, even in religion; the wisest and best instructed Christians are the most steady, and may be the most useful."

*Theology,* p. 385

"Partial knowledge is better than total ignorance. He who cannot get all he may wish must take heed to acquire all that he can."

*Theology,* p. 385

"Human learning, properly applied and sanctified by the divine Spirit, is of inconceivable benefit to a Christian minister in teaching and defending the truth of God."

*Theology,* p. 300

"The learning that is got from books, or the study of languages, is of little use to any man, and is of no estimation, unless practically applied to the purposes of life."

*Theology,* p. 300

"What a miserable preacher must he be who has all his divinity by study and learning, and nothing by experience!"

*Theology,* p. 314

"Even splendid natural abilities, adorned with human learning, can be no substitute for the gifts and graces of the Holy Spirit."

*Sermons,* 3:341

"Learning neither opens the eyes of the blind, nor converts souls. Even among ministers, we do not always find that the most learned are either the most holy or the most useful. Learning is good and useful . . . as a handmaid of religion, but it never did, and never can, convert a soul."

*Sermons,* 2:238

"The time is coming, and now is, when illiterate piety can do no more for the interest and permanency of the work of God than lettered irreligion did formerly."

Etheridge, p. 255

## Love

"A religion, the very essence of which is love, cannot suffer at its altars a heart that is revengeful and uncharitable, or which does not use its utmost endeavours to revive love in the heart of another."

*Theology*, p. 169

"God has many imitators of his power, independence, justice, etc., but few of his love, condescension, and kindness."

*Theology*, p. 169

## Ministers and Ministry

"While he is feeding others, he should take care to have his own soul fed: it is possible for a minister to be the instrument of feeding others, and yet starve himself."

*Theology*, p. 297

"Christian prudence should ever be connected with Christian zeal. It is a great work to bring sinners to Christ; it is a greater work to preserve them in the faith."

*Theology*, pp. 317-18

"He must be much in love with the cross who wishes to have his child a minister of the gospel; for, if he be such as God approves of in the work, his life will be a life of toil and suffering; he will be obliged to *sip*, at least, if not to drink largely of the cup of Christ."

*Theology*, p. 277

"He who boasts of his ancestry, talks of his mighty sacrifices, and insinuates that he has descended from much dignity, respectability, ease, and affluence, in order to become a Methodist preacher, is the character of which Mr. Wesley speaks, Rule 8. Such a one affects the gentleman, wishes to be thought so by others, may be thought so by persons as empty as himself; but, in the light of every man of good common sense, is a vain, conceited, empty ass; is unworthy of the ministry, should be cast out of the vineyard, and hooted from society."

*Theology*, p. 308

"Preach the law and its terrors to make way for the gospel of Christ crucified. But take heed, lest, while you announce the terrors of the Lord, in order to awaken sinners and prepare them for Christ, that you do not give way to your own spirit, especially if you meet with opposition."

*Theology,* pp. 308-9

"Avoid the error of those who are continually finding fault with their congregations because more do not attend. Bring Christ with you, and preach his truth in . . . love, . . . and you will never be without a congregation, if God have any work for you to do in that place."

*Theology,* p. 309

"Beware of discouraging the people; therefore, avoid continually finding fault with them. This does very much hurt."

*Theology,* p. 309

"And in humility, self-abasement, self-renunciation, and heavenly mindedness, they [ministers] are to be ensamples, types to the flock, moulds of a heavenly form, into which the spirits and lives of the flock may be cast, that they may come out after a perfect pattern."

*Theology,* p. 306

"There are to be no lords over God's heritage; the bishops and presbyters, who are appointed by the Head of the church, are to feed the flock, to guide and to defend it, not to fleece and waste it."

*Theology,* p. 306

"That minister who neglects the poor, but is frequent in his visits to the rich, knows little of his Master's work, and has little of his Master's spirit."

*Theology,* p. 305

"He will never send him to teach meekness, gentleness, and long suffering, who is proud, overbearing, intolerant, and impatient."

*Theology,* p. 301

Regarding a backslider: "When he was walking to heaven, I endeavoured to keep him in the way; and now that he is going to hell, I will endeavour to keep him out of it."

Everett, 2:96-97

## Music

"A good singer among the people of God, who has not the life of God in his soul, is *vox et praeterea nihil,* as Heliogabalus said of the nightingale's brains, on which he desired to sup, 'He is nothing but a sound.'"

*Theology,* p. 245

## Patience

"Persons of an over tender and scrupulous conscience may be very troublesome in a Christian society; but as this excessive scrupulosity comes from want of more light, more experience, or more judgment, we should bear with them. Though such should often run into ridiculous extremes, yet we must take care that we do not attempt to cure them either with ridicule or wrath."

*Theology,* p. 399

## Perseverance

"Whatever evil comes against me is an opposable evil—an evil that may be overcome."

*Sermons,* 4:246

"The vilest of the vile may change as long as he is in a state of probation. The holiest of the holy may fall, as long as he is in a state of probation."

*Sermons,* 4:72


"'Take heed lest ye fall.' I do contend there could not be any reason for the caution if that were impossible."

*Sermons,* 4:245


### Personal Religion
"If good and sound doctrine be not fully understood, it cannot be experienced; and if not experienced, it cannot be practiced; and if not brought into practice, it can be of no use. Hence [the need for] experimental, practical religion."

*Sermons,* 2:185


"A man who pretends to religion, and has no experimental knowledge of it, soon exposes himself. The words of it are not at all fitted in his lips. He knows not the principles of the language of Canaan—its grammar he has never learned—and to pretend to speak it, shows . . . ignorance . . . hypocrisy and folly."

*Sermons,* 2:186


"Learning I love. Learned men I prize. With the company of the great and good I am often delighted but infinitely above all these and all other enjoyments I glory in Christ in me living and reigning and fitting me for his heaven."

Everett, 1:308


"He who has not a tender conscience will not feel his continual need of divine help; and he who does not feel this need will not care for a supply; and he who does not

206

call for it, cannot be furnished with it, and must therefore fail in the day of battle."

*Sermons,* 1:118

"God alone can tell whom he has accepted . . . this he makes known by his Spirit in our spirit; so that we have, not by induction or inference, a thorough conviction and mental feeling that we are his children."

*Sermons,* 1:131

## Politics

"When preachers of the Gospel become parties in *party politics* religion mourns, the church is unedified, and political disputes agitate even the faithful."

J. B. B. Clarke, 1:154

## The Poor

"God has blessed those who have provided for the poor and needy, and he has given his promise, that he will help them in the time of trouble."

*Sermons,* 4:193

"I would give very little for that religion, which does not lead men to labour, in order to bring glory to God, and good to our fellow-creatures."

*Sermons,* 4:282

"What art thou, O rich man? Why, thou art a steward to whom God has given substance, that thou mayest divide with the poor. They are the right owners of every farthing thou hast to spare from thy own support and that of thy family; and God has given thee surplus for their sakes."

*Theology,* p. 287

"The abject poor, those who are destitute of health and the means of life, God in effect lays at the rich man's door, that by his superfluities they may be supported."

*Theology,* p. 288


## Prayer

"Prayer requires more of the heart than of the tongue."

*Theology,* p. 230


"Prayer is not designed to inform God, but to give man a sight of his misery; to humble his heart, to excite his desire, to inflame his faith, to animate his hope, to raise his soul from earth to heaven."

*Theology,* p. 230


"We must pray first to see what we need, and then we shall pray to get our wants supplied."

*Sermons,* 2:6


"The best I can wish for those who irreverently sit at prayer, is a porcupine skin for a cushion."

Everett, 2:58


"Faith in the declaration of God, firmly anchored in the heart, is a chain fastened to his throne; and by the constant exercise of which, we must endeavor to climb to heaven."

Everett, 2:2


"[God is] ever more ready to hear than we are to pray, and ever want to give more than we desire or deserve."

*Sermons,* 2:17


"All ministers, and others, who study to use fine expressions in their prayers, rather complimenting than praying to God, rank high among the hypocrites; and instead of being applauded by men, should be universally

208

abhorred. . . . That prayer which is the genuine effusion of a heart deeply impressed with its own necessities, and the presence of God, is invariably as simple as it is fervent and unostentatious."

*Sermons*, 2:9

"They who pray not, know nothing of this God, and know nothing of the state of their own souls."

*Sermons*, 2:137

## Preaching

"He who preaches the gospel as he ought, must do it with his whole strength of body and soul; and he who undertakes a labour of this kind thrice every Lord's day will infallibly shorten his life by it. He who, instead of preaching, talks to the people, merely speaks about good things, or tells a religious story, will never injure himself by such an employment; such a person does not labour in the word and doctrine; he tells his tale, and as he preaches, so his congregation believes, and sinners are left as he found them."

*Theology*, p. 323

"To enlighten the darkness and soften the hardness of the human heart, the energy of the Holy Spirit should accompany the preaching of the gospel. . . .

"It would be absurd for us to expect to do the same work without the Holy Ghost, which the apostles themselves could not do without it."

*Sermons*, 3:471

"It is worthy of remark, that in all the revivals of religion with which we are acquainted God appears to have made very little use of human eloquence, even when possessed by pious men. His own nervous truths, announced by plain common sense, though in homely phrase, have been the general means of the conviction and conversion of sinners. Human eloquence and learning have often been successfully employed in defending the outworks of Christianity; but simplicity and truth have preserved the citadel."

*Theology,* pp. 320-21

"He is not a seedsman of God who desires to sow by the wayside, and not on the proper ground; that is, he who loves to preach only to genteel congregations, to people of sense and fashion, and feels it a pain and a cross to labour among the poor and the ignorant."

*Theology,* p. 310

"Preach from your knowledge of God, from your experimental knowledge of divine things, from Christ dwelling in your heart by faith, from the cloven tongue of fire which God has given you; then your ministry will be tenfold more blessed than ever."

Everett, 2:218

"We seldom find great scholars good preachers. This should humble the scholar, who is too apt to be proud of his attainments, and despise his less learned but more useful brother."

*Theology,* p. 313

"Preaching merely hell-fire, as it is called, may alarm animal feelings and apprehensions; but if the mind be not convinced and impressed with a sense of its danger, there will be no radical awakening of the soul, nor preserving conversion of the heart to God."

*Sermons,* 3:270

"It is much to be lamented that the benevolent gospel of the Son of God is represented by many as a system of austerity and terror; but no man can represent it as such who understands it."

*Sermons,* 3:189

"From long experience I can testify, that preaching the love of Christ . . . is of more avail to convert sinners, comfort the distressed, and build up believers . . . than all the fire of hell. For as it is possible to make void the law, through a lawless method of preaching faith, so it is possible to make void the gospel by an unevangelized preaching of the law and its terrors."

*Sermons,* 3:189

"A dull, dead preacher makes a dull, dead congregation."

*Theology,* p. 325

"The only preaching worth any thing, in God's account, and which the fire will not burn up, is that which labours to convict and convince the sinner of his sin, to bring him into contrition for it, to convert him from it; to lead him to the blood of the covenant, that his conscience may be purged from its guilt,—to the Spirit of judgment and burning, that he may be purified from its infection,— and then to build him up on this most holy faith, by causing him to pray in the Holy Ghost, and keep himself in the love of God, looking for the mercy of our Lord Jesus Christ unto eternal life: this is the system pursued by the apostles, and it is that alone which God will own to the conversion of sinners. I speak from the experience of nearly fifty years in the public ministry of the word: this is the most likely mode to produce the active soul of divinity, while the body is little else but the preacher's creed."

*Theology,* p. 326

"In many cases, the success of a preacher's labours depends more on his prayers than on his public preaching."

*Sermons,* 3:174

"Preach Christ crucified: . . . By this alone are the drunkards, liars, sabbath-breakers, unclean, dishonest, and wicked of every class, converted . . . By this preaching, those who were pests of society, and a scandal to man, have become honest, upright, decent, orderly, industrious, holy, and useful."

*Sermons,* 2:237

### Pride
"Pride works frequently under a dense mask, and will often assume the garb of humility; how true is that saying . . .

> 'Proud I am my wants to see
> Proud of my humility.'"

*Sermons,* 3:285

"A proud man is peculiarly odious in the sight of God; and in the sight of reason how absurd! A sinner, a fallen spirit—an heir of wretchedness and corruption, proud! Proud of what? Of an indwelling devil! Well;—such persons shall be plentifully rewarded. They shall get their due, their whole due, and nothing but their due."

*Theology,* p. 181

"The affectation of wisdom is that in which man boasts beyond all other possessions."

*Sermons,* 2:368

## Providence

"There is not a circumstance in our life, not an occurrence in our business, but God will make subservient to our salvation, if we have a simple heart and teachable spirit."

*Theology,* p. 359

"By acting contrary to the divine counsel, we pierce ourselves through with many sorrows, and often provoke God, by our rebellion, we use that scheme of providence in opposition to us, which would have wrought together with his grace for our good, had we submitted ourselves in this direction."

J. B. B. Clarke, 2:133

"The world is full of evil and misery; and if I could believe that these were the result of divine counsels, and divine operations, I must also say, vain is the command to be happy, when by such evils the cup of blessedness is dashed from the lips of mortals, as frequently as they attempt to taste it: but I deny that God is the author of what is strictly styled evil."

*Sermons,* 1:233

## Repentance

"Learn that true repentance is a work, and not the work of an hour: it is not a passing regret, but a deep and alarming conviction, that thou art a fallen spirit, hast broken God's laws, art under the curse, and in danger of hell fire."

*Sermons,* 2:256

## Revenge

"He who avenges himself receives into his own heart all the evil and disgraceful passions by which his enemy is rendered both wretched and contemptible."

*Theology,* p. 173

## Riches

*"Riches* generally are a snare . . . because men are so prone to . . . forget their souls, while it is in their power to gratify their sensual appetites."

*Sermons,* 4:33

"Men often, by their perversity and attachment to sensible things, provoke divine justice to poison their enjoyments, and to curse their blessings."

*Sermons,* 4:34

"He who prays for RICHES, prays for snares, vanity, and vexation of spirit. He who prays for POVERTY, prays for what few can bear."

*Sermons,* 2:290

## Salvation by Faith

"Salvation by faith is a more simple, plain, easy doctrine, than one in a thousand imagines. That complexity and difficulty in which it is generally viewed, keep numbers from going up at once to possess the good land."

A letter to Mary

## Selfishness

"Self-interest is a most decisive casuist, and removes abundance of scruples in a moment. It is always the first consulted, and the most readily obeyed."

*Theology,* p. 423

"What a truly diabolic thing is the lust for power! It destroys all the charities of life, and renders those who are under its influence the truest resemblants of the arch fiend."

*Theology,* p. 421

# Sin

"So completely disgraceful is the way of sin, that, if there were not a multitude walking in that way, who help to keep each other in countenance, every solitary sinner would be obliged to hide his head."

*Theology*, p. 394

"We not only see the exceeding sinfulness of sin in the grandeur of the sacrifice required for its expiation; but we see also, in the dignity of the redeeming nature, the dignity of the nature to be redeemed."

*Sermons*, 2:455

"The sinner is not only unable to do any good thing, but he is totally indisposed to do it. To read the sacred writings he has no taste; to pray for his own salvation he has no disposition; to strive to enter in at the strait gate he has no energy."

*Sermons*, 1:181

"So deep is the stain, so radicated the habits of sinning, so strongly the propensity to . . . evil, that nothing less than the power by which the soul was created, can conquer these habits, eradicate these vices, and cause such a leopard to change his spots."

*Sermons*, 1:153

"Some seem to live only to invent schemes of sin, and bring to perfection the practice of transgression."

*Sermons*, 2:85

"There is a contagion in human nature, an evil principle, that is opposed to the truth and holiness of God. This is the grand hidden cause of all transgression. It is contagion from which no soul of man is free: it is propagated with the human species; no human being was ever born without it: it is the infection of our nature, is commonly called original sin,—sin, because it is without conformity to the nature, will, and law of God; and is constantly in opposition to all three."

*Theology,* p. 101

"Vice uncurbed daily gains strength."

*Sermons,* 1:107

"Sin must be an inconceivable evil, and possess an indescribable malignity, when it required no less a sacrifice to make atonement for it than that offered by God manifested in the flesh."

*Sermons,* 2:451

### Stewardship

"How liberal are many to public places of amusement, or to some popular charity, where their names are sure to be published abroad; while the man who watches over their souls is fed with the most parsimonious hand!"

*Theology,* pp. 330-31

"If the preachers of the gospel were as parsimonious of the bread of life as some congregations and Christian societies are of the bread that perisheth; and if the preacher gave them a spiritual nourishment as base, as mean, and as scanty as the temporal support which they afford him, their souls must, without doubt, have nearly a famine of the bread of life."

*Theology,* p. 330

"Look for your help to Him; do not suppose that any man's money is necessary to the support of Christ's cause. The earth is the Lord's and the fullness thereof."

Everett, 2:120

## Temperance

"He must have but a little religion and less sense, who does not see that he should be moderate in his food, sleep, clothing, domestic expenses, . . . and in everything that concerns him."

*Sermons,* 1:377

## Time

"Buy up those moments which others seem to throw away; steadily improve every present moment, that ye may, in some measure, regain the time ye have lost. Let time be your chief commodity; deal in that alone; buy it all up, and use every portion of it yourselves. Time is that on which eternity depends; in time ye are to get a preparation for the kingdom of God; if you get not this in time, your ruin is inevitable; therefore buy up the time."

*Theology,* p. 426

## War

"Is it not common for interested persons to rejoice in the successes of an unjust and sanguinary war, in the sackage and burning of cities and towns? and is not the joy always in proportion to the slaughter that has been made of the enemy? And do these call themselves Christians? Then we may expect that Moloch and his subdevils are not so far behind this description of Christians as to render their case utterly desperate. If such Christians can be saved, demons need not despair."

*Theology,* p. 176

## Witness

"The mere preaching of the gospel has done much to convince and convert sinners; but the lives of the sincere followers of Christ, as illustrative of the truth of these doctrines, have done much more."

*Theology,* p. 334

## Work

"He who wishes to save souls will find few opportunities to rest."

*Theology,* p. 317

## Worship

"He who can enter a place dedicated to the worship of God as he does into his own habitation or that of his horses has (in my opinion) no proper notion of religious worship, and is never likely to derive much edification from his attendance on the ordinances of God."

Etheridge, p. 266

# APPENDIX 1

| Theological Themes in Clarke's Preaching | Major Theme | Stressed Theme | Minor Theme | Raw Score | Rank |
|---|---|---|---|---|---|
| *Theology: Doctrine of God* | | | | | |
| Natural Theology | 1 | | 1 | 4 | |
| Attributes of God | 6 | 14 | 3 | 49 | |
| Creation | | 3 | | 6 | |
| Love and Grace of God | 14 | 6 | | 54 | 1 |
| Providence | 3 | 7 | 5 | 28 | |
| *Totals this category* | 24 | 30 | 9 | 141 | 2 |
| *Hamartiology/Anthropology: Doctrine of Man and Sin* | | | | | |
| Sinfulness of Man | 12 | 13 | 3 | 65 | 1 |
| Satan | | 1 | 1 | 3 | |
| Death | 1 | 1 | | 5 | |
| Doctrine of Man | 1 | 8 | 1 | 20 | |
| *Totals this category* | 14 | 23 | 5 | 93 | 3 |
| *Soteriology: Doctrine of Salvation* | | | | | |
| Adoption, Repentance, Regeneration | 4 | 4 | 1 | 21 | |
| Assurance | 2 | 5 | 3 | 19 | |
| Atonement | 11 | 14 | 1 | 62 | |
| Covenant/Law/Sacrifice | 2 | 4 | | 14 | |
| Justification/Pardon | 3 | 6 | 2 | 23 | |
| Sanctification | 17 | 15 | 6 | 87 | 1 |
| Salvation by Faith | 5 | 6 | 3 | 30 | |
| Heaven | 1 | 4 | 5 | 16 | |
| Hell | 1 | 2 | 5 | 12 | |
| Immortality | 1 | 1 | | 5 | |
| *Totals this category* | 47 | 61 | 26 | 289 | 1 |
| *Other Theological Themes* | | | | | |
| Revelation (scriptures) | 3 | 5 | 3 | 22 | |
| Christology | 4 | 6 | | 24 | 1 |
| False Doctrines/Religions | 1 | 4 | 2 | 13 | |
| Ecclesiology | | 3 | 4 | 10 | |
| Reason/Truth | 1 | 2 | | 7 | |
| Eschatology | | 1 | | 2 | |
| Sacraments | | | 1 | 1 | |
| *Totals this category* | 9 | 21 | 10 | 79 | 4 |

# APPENDIX 2

| Themes in Clarke's Preaching: Christian Life and Practice | Major Theme | Stressed Theme | Minor Theme | Raw Score | Rank |
|---|---|---|---|---|---|
| Call to Seek God | 4 | 16 | 15 | 59 | 2 |
| **Christian Attitudes** | | | | | |
| Love | 3 | | 1 | 10 | |
| Forgiveness | | 1 | | 2 | |
| Hope | 1 | | | 3 | |
| Happiness | 2 | 1 | | 8 | |
| Thanksgiving/Praise | 1 | 3 | | 9 | |
| Sincerity | 1 | | 1 | 4 | |
| Peace/Joy | 2 | 2 | 1 | 11 | 1 |
| *Totals this category* | 10 | 7 | 3 | 47 | 3 |
| *Christian Service* | 3 | 3 | | 15 | 10 |
| **Personal Discipleship** | | | | | |
| Prayer | 1 | 9 | 6 | 27 | 1 |
| Growth, Discipline, Obedience, etc. | 3 | 5 | 1 | 20 | |
| Temptation/Trials | 3 | 5 | 1 | 20 | |
| Perseverance | 2 | 3 | | 12 | |
| Bible Reading | | 1 | 2 | 4 | |
| Confession | | | 1 | 1 | |
| Decisionmaking | | 1 | 1 | 3 | |
| *Totals this category* | 9 | 24 | 12 | 87 | 1 |
| *Evangelism* | | | | | |
| Mission of Methodists | | 1 | | 2 | |
| Missions | 8 | 1 | 2 | 28 | |
| Preaching/Ministry | 2 | 1 | | 8 | 1 |
| Evangelism/Witnessing | | 2 | 1 | 5 | |
| *Totals this category* | 10 | 5 | 3 | 43 | 4 |
| **Experimental Religion** | | | | | |
| Religious Experience | 4 | 3 | 2 | 20 | 1 |
| Work of Holy Spirit | 2 | 1 | 1 | 9 | |
| Worship | 1 | 2 | | 7 | |
| *Totals this category* | 7 | 6 | 3 | 36 | 6 |
| **Faith and Trust** | | | | | |
| Anxiety, Worry | 1 | 2 | 1 | 8 | |
| Faith/Trust | 4 | 3 | 1 | 19 | 1 |
| *Totals this category* | 5 | 5 | 2 | 27 | 8 |

|  | Major Theme | Stressed Theme | Minor Theme | Raw Score | Rank |
|---|---|---|---|---|---|
| **The Holy Life** | | | | | |
| Holy Living | 5 | 8 | | 31 | 1 |
| Deliverance From All Sin | 1 | 2 | | 7 | |
| *Totals this category* | 6 | 10 | | 38 | 5 |
| **Specific Sins to Avoid** | | | | | |
| Backsliding | | 4 | | 8 | 1 |
| Idolatry | | 2 | 1 | 5 | |
| Lying/Slander | | | 3 | 3 | |
| Quarrelling | | 2 | | 4 | |
| Worldliness | | 2 | 1 | 5 | |
| Pride/Vanity | | 1 | | 2 | |
| Drunkenness | | | 2 | 2 | |
| *Totals this category* | | 11 | 7 | 29 | 7 |
| **Stewardship** | | | | | |
| Money | | 8 | 1 | 17 | 1 |
| Work | | 1 | 2 | 4 | |
| *Totals this category* | | 9 | 3 | 21 | 9 |

# APPENDIX 3
## Adam Clarke's Old Testament Quotations

| Book | Number of Texts from This Book | Quoted When Used as the Text | Quoted When Not a Text | Total Quotations |
|---|---|---|---|---|
| **Pentateuch:** | | | | |
| Genesis | 0 | 0 | 66 | 66 |
| Exodus | 1 | 31 | 6 | 37 |
| Leviticus | 0 | 0 | 4 | 4 |
| Numbers | 0 | 0 | 3 | 3 |
| Deuteronomy | 0 | 0 | 14 | 14 |
| Unidentified Law | | | 1 | 1 |
| *Totals for Pentateuch* | 1 | 31 | 94 | 125 |
| **Historical Books:** | | | | |
| Joshua | 0 | 0 | 3 | 3 |
| Judges | 0 | 0 | 3 | 3 |
| 1 & 2 Samuel | 1 | 14 | 5 | 19 |
| 1 & 2 Kings | 1 | 15 | 4 | 19 |
| 1 & 2 Chronicles | 0 | 0 | 2 | 2 |
| *Totals for Historical Books* | 2 | 29 | 17 | 46 |
| **Wisdom Literature:** | | | | |
| Job | 1 | 19 | 12 | 31 |
| Psalms | 6 | 114 | 44 | 158 |
| Proverbs | 2 | 43 | 9 | 52 |
| Ecclesiastes | 0 | 0 | 9 | 9 |
| *Totals for Wisdom Literature* | 9 | 176 | 74 | 250 |
| **Prophets:** | | | | |
| Isaiah | 2 | 7 | 37 | 44 |
| Jeremiah | 1 | 1 | 8 | 9 |
| Ezekiel | 0 | 0 | 10 | 10 |
| Daniel | 1 | 6 | 11 | 17 |
| Hosea | 0 | 0 | 5 | 5 |
| Joel | 1 | 9 | 1 | 10 |
| Amos | 0 | 0 | 6 | 6 |
| Jonah | 0 | 0 | 1 | 1 |
| Micah | 0 | 0 | 4 | 4 |
| Habakkuk | 1 | 1 | 0 | 1 |
| Zechariah | 0 | 0 | 4 | 4 |
| Malachi | 0 | 0 | 5 | 5 |
| Unidentified Prophet | 0 | 0 | 5 | 5 |
| *Totals from the Prophets* | 6 | 24 | 97 | 121 |
| *Grand Totals* | 18 | 260 | 282 | 542 |

Average number of Old Testament quotes per sermon: 9.03

Average number of references (quotes) to the text per Old Testament sermon: 14.44

222

# APPENDIX 4
## Adam Clarke's New Testament Quotations

| Book | Number of Texts from This Book | Quoted When Used as the Text | Quoted When Not the Text | Total Quotations |
|---|---|---|---|---|
| **Gospels:** | | | | |
| Matthew | 6 | 62 | 52 | 114 |
| Mark | 0 | 0 | 8 | 8 |
| Luke | 3 | 30 | 16 | 46 |
| Unidentified Synoptic | | | 49 | 49 |
| John | 4 | 34 | 59 | 93 |
| *Totals for All Gospels* | 13 | 126 | 184 | 310 |
| **Acts:** | 3 | 21 | 70 (40 in one sermon) | 91 |
| **Pauline Epistles:** | | | | |
| Romans | 3 | 17 | 53 | 70 |
| 1 & 2 Corinthians | 4 | 41 | 44 | 85 |
| Galatians | 2 | 13 | 13 | 26 |
| Ephesians | 1 | 20 | 33 | 53 |
| Philippians | 5 | 45 | 8 | 53 |
| Colossians | 1 | 15 | 14 | 29 |
| 1 & 2 Thessalonians | 1 | 5 | 3 | 8 |
| 1 & 2 Timothy | 1 | 4 | 22 | 26 |
| Titus | 0 | 0 | 8 | 8 |
| Unidentified Pauline | 0 | 0 | 26 | 26 |
| *Totals for Pauline Epistles* | 18 | 160 | 224 | 384 |
| **General Epistles:** | | | | |
| Hebrews | 3 | 21 | 40 | 61 |
| James | 1 | 2 | 5 | 7 |
| 1 & 2 Peter | 4 | 45 | 32 | 77 |
| 1 John | 2 | 32 | 23 | 55 |
| Jude | 0 | 0 | 6 | 6 |
| *Totals for General Epistles* | 10 | 100 | 106 | 206 |
| **Revelation:** | 0 | 0 | 22 | 22 |
| *Grand Total New Testament* | 44 | 407 | 606 | 1,013 |
| Pauline Literature | 18 | 160 | 224 | 384 |
| Synoptic Gospels | 9 | 92 | 125 | 217 |
| Johannine Literature | 6 | 66 | 104 | 170 |
| Petrine Literature | 4 | 45 | 32 | 77 |

Average number of New Testament quotes per sermon: 16.88

Average number of references to text per New Testament sermon: 9.25

# APPENDIX 5

**Readability of Clarke's Sermons**

| Edited Sermons | Number of Words in Sample | Number of Sentences in Sample | Number of Words Not on Dale List | Average Number of Words per Sentence | Dale Score | Raw Score | Grade Level |
|---|---|---|---|---|---|---|---|
| Sample I<br>Introduction<br>Sermon 4 | 109 | 3 | 22 | 36 | 20.18 | 8.58 | 12 |
| Sample II<br>Introduction<br>Sermon 16 | 110 | 3 | 19 | 40 | 15.96 | 8.15 | 11 |
| Sample III<br>Conclusion<br>Sermon 22 | 108 | 6 | 18 | 18 | 16.66 | 7.37 | 9 |
| Sample IV<br>Conclusion<br>Sermon 31 | 108 | 3 | 13 | 36 | 12.0 | 7.32 | 9 |
| Sample V<br>Body<br>Sermon 34 | 102 | 3 | 28 | 34 | 27.4 | 9.59 | 14 |
| Sample VI<br>Sermon 35 | 110 | 3 | 15 | 34 | 14.8 | 7.69 | 10 |
| Sample VII<br>Sermon 42 | 119 | 5 | 22 | 24 | 18.4 | 7.67 | 10 |
| Sample VIII<br>Sermon 1 | 133 | 5 | 19 | 27 | 14.2 | 7.19 | 9 |
| Sample IX<br>Sermon 25 | 126 | 5 | 26 | 25 | 20.6 | 8.19 | 11 |
| Sample X<br>Sermon 44 | 110 | 5 | 17 | 22 | 15.4 | 7.10 | 9 |
| *Subtotals*<br>*Edited Sermons* | 1,135 | 41 | 199 | 27.7 | 17.53 | 7.87 | 10 |

| Shorthand Sermons | Number of Words in Sample | Number of Sentences in Sample | Number of Words Not on Dale List | Average Number of Words per Sentence | Dale Score | Raw Score | Grade Level |
|---|---|---|---|---|---|---|---|
| Sample XI Introduction Sermon 46 (1815) | 125 | 3 | 8 | 42 | 6.4 | 6.67 | 8 |
| Sample XII Conclusion Sermon 51 (1820) | 108 | 6 | 13 | 18 | 12.0 | 6.42 | 7 |
| Sample XIII Body Sermon 52 (1818) | 122 | 3 | 21 | 41 | 17.2 | 8.37 | 11 |
| Sample XIV Sermon 64 (1832) | 115 | 8 | 16 | 14 | 13.9 | 6.54 | 8 |
| Sample XV Body Sermon 55 (1816) | 111 | 6 | 23 | 19 | 20.7 | 7.89 | 10 |
| *Subtotals Shorthand Sermons* | 581 | 26 | 81 | 22 | 13.9 | 6.94 | 8 |
| *Grand Totals* | 1,716 | 67 | 280 | 25.6 | 16.3 | 7.40 | 9 |

# Reference Notes

INTRODUCTION:

1. Maldwyn L. Edwards, *Adam Clarke* (London: Epworth Press, The Wesley Historical Society Lectures, No. 8, 1942), p. 45.

CHAPTER 1:

1. James Everett, *Adam Clarke Portrayed*, 2nd ed. (London: W. Reed, 1866), 1:300.

2. James Everett, in the "General Preface" to *Discourses on Various Subjects Relative to the Being and Attributes of God and His Works in Creation, Providence, and Grace* (hereafter referred to as *Sermons*), 4 vols. (London: Wm. Tegg, 1868), 1:xxxviii.

3. J. W. Etheridge, *The Life of the Rev. Adam Clarke, LL.D.* (Nashville: Southern Methodist Publishing House, 1859), p. 23.

4. Ibid.

5. Everett, *Adam Clarke Portrayed*, 1:32.

6. Ibid.

7. Ibid.

8. Ibid.

9. J. B. B. Clarke, ed., *An Account of the Infancy, Religious and Literary Life of Adam Clarke, LL.D., F.A.S., Etc.*, 3 vols. in 1 (New York: B. Waugh and T. Mason, 1833), 1:16.

10. Samuel Dunn, ed., *Christian Theology by Adam Clarke, LL.D., F.A.S., from His Published and Unpublished Writings and Systematically Arranged: With a Life of the Author* (Salem, Ohio: H. E. Schmul, 1967), p. 10.

11. Everett, *Adam Clarke Portrayed*, 1:25.

12. Quoted by Etheridge, *Adam Clarke*, pp. 35-36.

13. Ibid., p. 31.

14. Ibid., p. 32.

15. Ibid.

16. J. B. B. Clarke, *Adam Clarke,* 1:36.

17. Ibid.

18. Ibid., p. 47.

19. Quoted by Etheridge, *Adam Clarke,* pp. 48-49.

20. J. B. B. Clarke, *Adam Clarke,* 3:77-78.

21. Ibid., 1:82.

22. Ibid., p. 83.

23. Ibid.

24. Etheridge, *Adam Clarke,* p. 73.

25. Everett, *Adam Clarke Portrayed,* 2:100.

26. Ibid., pp. 292-93.

27. Ibid., 1:175.

28. Etheridge, *Adam Clarke,* p. 353.

29. From a letter to his sister, Everett, *Adam Clarke Portrayed,* 1:163.

30. Elden Dale Dunlap, "Methodist Theology in Great Britain in the Nineteenth Century" (Ph.D. diss., Yale University, 1956), p. 75.

31. Ibid.

32. Ibid., p. 77.

33. The volumes published posthumously as sermons contained 64 discourses, but four of these cannot properly be called sermons. One was a tract, another a short book, and two others were speeches made on special occasions. In this book only the 60 sermons, properly so called, are analyzed.

34. *The Triumphs of\ Industry; Illustrated by the Life of Adam Clarke, LL.D.* (Philadelphia: American Sunday School Union, 1854), p. 202.

35. Edwards, *Adam Clarke,* p. 28.

36. *Triumphs of Industry,* p. 202.

CHAPTER 2:

1. Dunn, *Clarke's Theology,* p. 40.

2. Ibid., p. 37.

3. Etheridge, *Adam Clarke,* p. 197.

4. *Triumphs of Industry,* p. 203.

5. Etheridge, *Adam Clarke,* p. 199.

6. Everett, "General Preface" to the *Sermons,* 1:xxii, xxvii.

7. Ibid., p. xxvii.

8. Dunn, *Clarke's Theology,* pp. 39, 42.

9. Etheridge, *Adam Clarke,* p. 197.

10. Everett, *Adam Clarke Portrayed,* 1:266.

11. Ibid., 2:115.

12. Dunn, *Clarke's Theology*, p. 42.

13. *Triumphs of Industry*, p. 206.

14. Etheridge, *Adam Clarke*, p. 199.

15. J. B. B. Clarke, *Adam Clarke*, 3:243.

16. Etheridge, *Adam Clarke*, p. 201.

17. *Triumphs of Industry*, p. 201.

18. See J. B. B. Clarke, *Adam Clarke*, 3:240; Dunn, *Christian Theology*, p. 32; and *The Triumphs of Industry*, p. 197, for descriptions of Clarke's appearance.

19. *Triumphs of Industry*, p. 198.

20. Everett, *Adam Clarke Portrayed*, 2:29.

21. Dunn, *Clarke's Theology*, pp. 40-41.

22. Donald E. Demaray, *Proclaiming the Truth* (Grand Rapids: Baker Book House, 1979), p. 98.

23. Quoted by Dunn, *Clarke's Theology*, p. 324.

24. *Triumphs of Industry*, p. 122.

25. Everett, *Adam Clarke Portrayed*, 1:121.

26. *Triumphs of Industry*, p. 206.

27. Etheridge, *Adam Clarke*, p. 201.

28. Everett, "General Preface" to the *Sermons*, 1:xxx.

29. J. B. B. Clarke, *Adam Clarke*, 3:242-43.

CHAPTER 3:

1. "On the Being and Attributes of God," *Sermons*, 1:12.

2. "Acquaintance with God," *Sermons*, 2:129.

3. "The Doctrine of Holiness," *Sermons*, 4:108.

4. Ibid., p. 103.

5. *Triumphs of Industry*, pp. 122-23.

6. "Paul's Glorying," *Sermons*, 4:150.

7. "The Love of God to Man," *Sermons*, 4:117-18.

8. Ibid., p. 119.

9. Ibid., p. 121.

10. "Experimental Religion and Its Fruits," *Sermons*, 1:133; also "The Love of God to a Lost World," 4:183; "Prophecy Fulfilled in Christ," 4:98, and other places.

11. "The Family of God and Its Privileges," *Sermons*, 1:307.

12. *Triumphs of Industry*, p. 116.

13. "The Love of God to Man," *Sermons*, 2:176.

14. "Life the Gift of the Gospel, Love the Ministration of Death," *Sermons*, 1:209.

15. "The Characteristic Affection and Prime Objects of the Christian Ministry," *Sermons*, 4:296.

16. "The Christian Prophet and His Work," *Sermons*, 3:174.

17. Ibid.

18. "Acquaintance with God," *Sermons*, 2:137.

19. "Saint Peter's Character of the Dispersed Among the Gentiles," *Sermons*, 3:342.

20. "Probation and Temptation," *Sermons*, 4:246, 251.

21. "Experimental Religion and Its Fruits," *Sermons*, p. 131.

22. Ibid., pp. 130-31.

23. "The Wise Man's Counsels to His People," *Sermons*, 2:186.

24. "Genuine Happiness the Privilege of the Christian in This Life," *Sermons*, 1:245.

CHAPTER 4:

1. James Everett, *Adam Clarke Portrayed*, 2:277.

2. "Apostolic Preaching," *Sermons*, 3:262.

3. "St. Peter's Character of the Dispersed Among the Gentiles and His Prayer for a Multiplication of Grace and Peace in the Church of God," *Sermons*, 3:343.

4. "An Introduction to the Four Gospels and to the Acts of the Apostles," *Clarke's Commentary* (New York: Abingdon, n.d.), 5:10.

5. See *Christian Theology*, ed. Samuel Dunn; the "Introduction" in vol. 5 of the *Commentary;* and his sermon on "Divine Revelation" for Clarke's full treatment of inspiration.

6. "Divine Revelation," *Sermons*, 2:398, 399, 420.

7. *Clarke's Commentary*, 5:13.

8. "The Wisdom That Is from Above," *Sermons*, 1:217.

9. "St. Peter's Character of the Dispersed Among the Gentiles," *Sermons*, 3:332. See also *Sermons*, 4:69 and 284.

10. "Introduction," *Commentary*, 5:14.

11. "The Love of God to Man," *Sermons*, 4:126-27.

12. "The Love of God to a Lost World," *Sermons*, 4:168.

13. Everett, *Adam Clarke Portrayed*, 2:362.

14. J. B. B. Clarke, *Adam Clarke*, 3:242.

15. "Two Important Questions Answered," *Sermons*, 2:99.

16. Ibid., p. 121.

17. "The Lord's Prayer," *Sermons*, 2:3-4.

18. "Two Important Questions Answered," *Sermons*, 2:120.

CHAPTER 5:

1. Roy Short, quoted by Lloyd Perry and John Strubhar in *Evangelistic Preaching* (Chicago: Moody Press, 1979), p. 77.

2. Robert I. Sumner, quoted by Perry and Strubhar, p. 79.

3. "The Necessity of Christ's Atonement," *Sermons*, 4:141.

4. Ibid., pp. 149-50.

5. "The Rich Man and the Beggar," *Sermons*, 4:28.

6. "The Doctrine of Holiness," *Sermons*, 4:100.

7. "The God of All Grace," *Sermons*, 4:229-30.

8. "The Christian Race," *Sermons*, 4:274.

9. "God's Entreaty to Sinners," *Sermons*, 4:385.

10. "The Corruption That Is in the World Through Lust," *Sermons*, 2:382.


CHAPTER 6:

1. I. Benson and M. Prosser, ed., *Readings in Classical Rhetoric* (Bloomington, Ind.: University of Indiana Press, 1969), p. 57.

2. Ibid., p. 118.

3. W. F. Jabusch, *The Person in the Pulpit* (Nashville: Abingdon, 1980), pp. 13-14.

4. Etheridge, *Adam Clarke*, p. 202.

5. *Triumphs of Industry*, p. 206.

6. Everett, "General Preface" to the *Sermons*, 1:xlii.

7. Etheridge, *Adam Clarke*, pp. 199-200.

8. Quoted by Merrill S. Williams in "Anointing: Preaching Isn't Preaching Without It," *The Preacher's Magazine*, Vol. 56, No. 1, p. 48.

9. Ibid., p. 49.

10. J. B. B. Clarke, *Adam Clarke*, p. 185.

11. Etheridge, *Adam Clarke*, p. 76.

12. Quoted by Etheridge, ibid., p. 83.

13. Everett, "General Preface" to the *Sermons*, 1:xxxviii.

14. Etheridge, *Adam Clarke*, p. 194.

15. Ibid., p. 190.


CHAPTER 7:

1. John Gerrung, quoted by Perry and Strubhar in *Evangelistic Preaching*, p. 34.

2. Raymond W. McLaughlin, *Communication in the Church* (Grand Rapids: Zondervan Publishing House, 1968), p. 12.

3. Demaray, *Proclaiming the Truth*, p. 29.

4. *Sermons*, 2:156.

5. *Sermons*, 1:142.

6. *Sermons*, 2:298.

7. David H. C. Read, *Sent from God: The Enduring Power and Mystery of Preaching* (Nashville: Abingdon, 1974), p. 105.

8. Sometimes points (1) and (2) are reversed.

9. *Sermons*, 1:57 ff.

10. "The Encouragement and Condescending Entreaty of God to Sinners," *Sermons*, vol. 4.

11. *Sermons*, 1:138-39.

12. Edwards, *Adam Clarke*, p. 28.

13. Ibid., p. 29.


CHAPTER 8:

1. Leslie Thonssen, A. Craig Baird, Waldo Braden, *Speech Criticism* (New York: Ronald Press, 1970), p. 515.

2. Wallace E. Fisher, *Who Dares to Preach?* (Minneapolis: Augsburg Publishing House, 1979), p. 167.

3. Henry Sloane Coffin, quoted by Perry and Strubhar, *Evangelistic Preaching*, p. 125.

4. Cited by Thonssen et al., *Speech Criticism*, p. 487.

5. Quoted by Thonssen et al., ibid., p. 498.

6. "The Doctrine of Repentance," *Sermons*, 4:407.

7. Aristotle, *The Rhetoric*, trans. Lane Cooper (New York: Appleton-Century-Crofts, 1960), p. 216.

8. Quoted by Thonssen et al., *Speech Criticism*, p. 498

9. Everett, *Adam Clarke Portrayed*, 2:108.

10. Etheridge, *Adam Clarke*, p. 326.

11. *Triumphs of Industry*, p. 205.

12. Everett, *Adam Clarke Portrayed*, 2:133.

13. Aristotle, *The Rhetoric* (Cooper), p. 191.

14. "Christ Crucified," *Sermons*, 2:230.

15. G. F. Quackenbos, *Composition and Rhetoric* (1862), quoted by Thonssen et al., *Speech Criticism*, p. 493.

16. Etheridge, *Adam Clarke*, p. 188.

17. John A. Broadus, *On the Preparation and Delivery of Sermons* (New York: Charlotte E. Broadus, 1898), p. 361.

18. Al Fasol, comp., *Selected Readings in Preaching* (Grand Rapids: Baker Book House, 1979), p. 124.

19. Sheridan Baker, *The Complete Stylist*, 2nd ed. (New York: Thomas Y. Crowell Co., 1972), p. 112.

20. *Sermons,* 3:276.

21. Ibid., 2:271.

22. Ibid., p. 72.

23. Ibid., 4:131.

24. Ibid., 2:104.

25. Ibid., 3:431.

26. Ibid., 4:259.

27. Ibid., pp. 334-35.

28. Ibid., 1:54.

29. Ibid., p. 160.

30. Ibid., 3:339.

31. Quoted by Baker, *The Complete Stylist,* p. 382.

32. *Sermons,* 3:438.

33. Ibid., p. 423.

34. Ibid., 2:32.

35. Ibid., 1:276.

36. Ibid., p. 340.

37. Ibid., 2:284.

38. Ibid., 1:99.

39. Baker, *The Complete Stylist,* pp. 385-86.

40. *Sermons,* 4:164.

41. Ibid., p. 359.

42. Ibid., p. 164.

43. Ibid., 2:284.

44. Baker, *The Complete Stylist,* p. 379.

45. "Two Important Questions Answered," *Sermons,* 2:120.

46. Fisher, *Who Dares to Preach?,* p. 163.

CHAPTER 9:

1. "Apostolic Preaching," *Sermons,* 3:267.

2. Ibid.

3. "The Doctrine of Repentance," *Sermons,* 4:395.

4. Ibid.

5. "Apostolic Preaching," *Sermons,* 3:292.

6. "The Necessity of Christ's Atonement," *Sermons,* 4:140-41.

7. Dunn, *Clarke's Theology,* p. 199.

8. "God's Love in Christ," *Sermons,* 4:372.

9. "The Love of God to a Lost World," *Sermons,* 2:445.

10. Ibid., p. 444.

11. "The Corruption That Is in the World Through Lust," *Sermons,* 2:369.

12. Quoted by Everett, *Adam Clarke Portrayed*, 2:14.

13. "Apostolic Preaching," *Sermons*, 3:277.

14. "The Love of God to a Lost World," *Sermons*, 2:451.

15. "Christ Crucified," *Sermons*, 2:235.

16. Quoted by Clarke in "The Love of God to a Lost World," *Sermons*, 2:450.

17. "Genuine Happiness the Privilege of the Christian in This Life," *Sermons*, 1:251.

18. "The Necessity of Christ's Atonement," *Sermons*, 4:155.

19. "The Wisdom That Is from Above," *Sermons*, 1:220.

20. "The Love of God to a Lost World," *Sermons*, 2:470.

21. Ibid., p. 469.

22. "The Wisdom That Is from Above," *Sermons*, 1:221.

23. "Genuine Happiness," *Sermons*, 1:246-47.

24. "The Love to God and Man," *Sermons*, 2:179.

25. "The Love of God to a Lost World," *Sermons*, 2:469.

26. "The Family of God and Its Privileges," *Sermons*, 1:309-10.

27. "Two Important Questions Answered," *Sermons*, 2:121.

28. "The Family of God," *Sermons*, 1:310.

29. "The Encouragement and Condescending Entreaty of God to Sinners," *Sermons*, 4:318.

30. "The Family of God," *Sermons*, 1:294.

31. "Genuine Happiness," *Sermons*, 1:245.

32. "The Love of God to a Lost World," *Sermons*, 2:470.

33. "Experimental Religion and Its Fruits," *Sermons*, 1:124.

34. "The Corruption That Is in the World Through Lust," *Sermons*, 2:362.

35. "The Necessity of Christ's Atonement," *Sermons*, 4:154.

36. "The Love of God to Man," *Sermons*, 4:120-21.

37. "The Family of God," *Sermons*, 1:309.

38. "Life, the Gift of the Gospel, The Law the Ministration of Death," *Sermons*, 1:204.

39. "The Corruption That Is in the World Through Lust," *Sermons*, 2:381.

40. "The Lord's Prayer," *Sermons*, 2:21.

41. "The Design and Use of the Jewish Sacrifices," *Sermons*, 2:80.

42. "The Plan of Human Redemption," *Sermons*, 1:80.

43. Letter to John Wesley, quoted by J. W. Etheridge, *Adam Clarke*, p. 503.

44. "Salvation by Faith," *Sermons*, 3:129.

45. "The Love of God to a Lost World," *Sermons*, 2:469.

46. "The Corruption That Is in the World Through Lust," *Sermons*, 2:382.

47. "The Disease and Cure of Naaman," *Sermons*, 1:179.

48. "The Love to God and Man," *Sermons*, 2:174, 176.

49. Ibid., p. 165.

50. "The Doctrine of Holiness," *Sermons*, 4:113.

51. "The Gift of a Savior the Fulfillment of Prophecy," *Sermons*, 4:97-98.

52. "The Love to God and Man," *Sermons*, 2:167.

53. "The Doctrine of Holiness," *Sermons*, 4:113.

54. "Genuine Happiness," *Sermons*, 1:245.

55. Ibid.

56. Dunn, *Clarke's Theology*, p. 175.

57. "Apostolic Preaching," *Sermons*, 3:282.

58. "The Plan of Human Redemption," *Sermons*, 1:80.

59. "Christ Crucified," *Sermons*, 2:236.

60. "The Hope of the Gospel," *Sermons*, 1:361.

61. "The Wisdom That Is from Above," *Sermons*, 1:221.

62. "The Doctrine of Repentance," *Sermons*, 4:395.

63. "The Family of God," *Sermons*, 1:283.

64. "Genuine Happiness," *Sermons*, 1:436.

65. "Experimental Religion," *Sermons*, 1:134.

66. Dunn, *Clarke's Theology*, p. 201.

67. "Salvation by Faith," *Sermons*, 3:166.

68. "Promises to the Man Who Has Set His Love upon God," *Sermons*, 4:260.

69. "The Doctrine of Repentance," *Sermons*, 4:386.

70. "The Corruption That Is in the World Through Lust," *Sermons*, 2:384-85.

CHAPTER 10:

1. This event is a dramatization of events which were said by Clarke's biographers to happen more than once.

2. Everett, *Adam Clarke Portrayed*, 1:300.

3. "God's Love in Christ," *Sermons*, 4:384.

4. Everett, *Adam Clarke Portrayed*, 2:101.

5. "Probation and Temptation," *Sermons*, 4:250.

6. Dunn, *Clarke's Theology*, pp. 170-71.

7. "The History of the Rich Man and the Beggar," *Sermons*, 4:24-25.

8. "The Lord's Prayer," *Sermons*, 2:29.

9. Ibid., p. 28.

10. J. B. B. Clarke, *Adam Clarke*, 1:117.

11. Everett, *Adam Clarke Portrayed*, 1:117.

12. Ibid.

13. J. B. B. Clarke, *Adam Clarke*, 3:209.

14. "The Encouragement and Condescending Entreaty of God to Sinners," *Sermons*, 4:324.

15. "Confidence in God, And Its Reward," *Sermons*, 4:77.

16. "The High Commission," *Sermons*, 4:464.

17. "The Prayer of Agur," *Sermons*, 2:286.

18. "History of the Rich Man and the Beggar," *Sermons*, 4:8.

19. Everett, *Adam Clarke Portrayed*, 1:190.

20. Ibid., p. 194.

21. Ibid., pp. 194-95.

22. Dunn, *Clarke's Theology*, p. 424.

23. J. B. B. Clarke, *Adam Clarke*, 3:126.

24. Ibid., pp. 126-27.

25. "God's Love in Jesus Christ, Considered in Its Objects, Its Freeness, and Saving Results," *Sermons*, 4:391.

26. *Adam Clarke Portrayed*, 2:100.

27. Etheridge, *Adam Clarke*, p. 442.

28. "The Necessity of Christ's Atonement," *Sermons*, 4:164.

29. Everett, *Adam Clarke Portrayed*, 2:67.

30. Ibid., 1:299.

31. Ibid., pp. 75-76.

32. Ibid., p. 76.

33. "The Love of God to Man," *Sermons*, 2:172.

CHAPTER 11:

1. J. B. B. Clarke, *Adam Clarke*, 3:221.

2. "Letter to a Preacher," quoted by Dunn, *Clarke's Theology*, p. 292.

3. *Sermons*, 3:472.

4. "Letter to a Preacher," Dunn, *Clarke's Theology*, p. 294.

5. Ibid., p. 307.

6. Ibid., p. 303.

7. Ibid., p. 307.

8. Ibid., p. 293.

9. Ibid., p. 295.

10. Ibid., p. 293.

11. Ibid., p. 295.
12. Ibid., p. 296.
13. Ibid., p. 300.
14. Ibid., p. 311.
15. Ibid., p. 323.
16. J. B. B. Clarke, *Adam Clarke*, 1:74.
17. Ibid., p. 75.
18. Ibid.
19. Everett, *Adam Clarke Portrayed*, 1:192.
20. J. B. B. Clarke, *Adam Clarke*, 3:235.
21. Everett, *Adam Clarke Portrayed*, 2:179.
22. Etheridge, *Adam Clarke*, p. 525.
23. J. B. B. Clarke, *Adam Clarke*, 2:172.
24. "The Lord's Prayer," *Sermons*, 2:7.
25. Etheridge, *Adam Clarke*, p. 519.
26. *Sermons*, 3:273.
27. J. B. B. Clarke, *Adam Clarke*, 3:177.
28. "Christian Moderation," *Sermons*, 1:375.
29. Etheridge, *Adam Clarke*, p. 507.

CHAPTER 12:

1. J. B. B. Clarke, *Adam Clarke*, 3:211.
2. Ibid., p. 221.
3. Ibid.
4. Ibid.
5. Ibid.
6. Edwards, *Adam Clarke*, p. 44.
7. Everett, *Adam Clarke Portrayed*, 2:247.
8. "The Different Methods God Has Used to Bring Men to the Knowledge of Himself," *Sermons*, 1:321.
9. John Wesley, "A Letter to the Reverend John Taylor, D.D.," *The Works of John Wesley*, 3rd ed. (Kansas City: Beacon Hill Press of Kansas City, 1978), 9:465.
10. Wesley, *Works*, 6:223.
11. Dunn, *Clarke's Theology*, p. 94.
12. Ibid., p. 95.
13. Ibid.
14. Ibid., p. 99.
15. Ibid., p. 98.
16. Ibid., p. 101.
17. "The Love of God to a Lost World," *Sermons*, 2:449.
18. Dunn, *Clarke's Theology*, p. 110.

19. "The Plan of Human Redemption," *Sermons,* 1:63-64.

20. "Salvation by Faith," *Sermons,* 3:162.

21. "The Encouragement and Condescending Entreaty of God to Sinners," *Sermons,* 4:317.

22. Wesley, *Works,* 10:349.

23. Wesley, *Works,* 7:317.

24. William R. Cannon, *The Theology of John Wesley* (Nashville: Abingdon, 1956), p. 82.

25. Ibid., p. 103.

26. "The God of All Grace," *Sermons,* 2:234.

27. "The Gift of a Savior," *Sermons,* 4:95.

28. "The God of All Grace," *Sermons,* 2:231.

29. Dunn, *Clarke's Theology,* p. 139.

30. Cannon, *Theology of John Wesley,* p. 216.

31. Everett, *Adam Clarke Portrayed,* 2:316.

32. Wesley, "The Witness of the Spirit," *Works,* 5:114.

33. Dunn, *Clarke's Theology,* p. 152.

34. *Sermons,* 1:130-31.

35. *Sermons,* 2:385.

36. Dunn, *Clarke's Theology,* p. 375.

37. "Design and Use of the Jewish Sacrifices," *Sermons,* 2:242.

38. "Death Unavoidable," *Sermons,* 2:79.

39. Dunn, *Clarke's Theology,* p. 377.

40. Ibid., p. 378.

41. "The Family of God and Its Privileges," *Sermons,* 1:294.

42. Ibid., p. 295.

43. "The Corruption That Is in the World Through Lust," *Sermons,* 2:382.

44. "The History of the Rich Man and the Beggar," *Sermons,* 4:13.

45. "Design and Use of the Jewish Sacrifices," *Sermons,* 2:252.

46. Everett, *Adam Clarke Portrayed,* 2:39.

47. "Love to God and Man," *Sermons,* 2:172.

48. Ibid., p. 193.

49. Everett, *Adam Clarke Portrayed,* 2:253.

50. Jeremy C. Jackson, *No Other Foundation* (Westchester, Ill.: Cornerstone Books, 1980), p. 192.

51. "The Necessity of Christ's Atonement," *Sermons,* 4:159.

52. Adam Clarke, in a letter to his wife, Mary, quoted in J. B. B. Clarke, *Adam Clarke,* 3:61.

237

53. Ibid., p. 192.

54. This poem was written by Dr. J. Kenneth Grider after hearing an address about Clarke made by the author of this book. It is used with Dr. Grider's permission.